NORTH

LEADERS OF THE CIVIL WAR ERA

Harriet Beecher Stowe

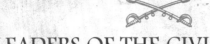

LEADERS OF THE CIVIL WAR ERA

John Brown

Jefferson Davis

Frederick Douglass

Ulysses S. Grant

Stonewall Jackson

Robert E. Lee

Abraham Lincoln

William Tecumseh Sherman

Harriet Beecher Stowe

Harriet Tubman

LEADERS OF THE CIVIL WAR ERA

Harriet Beecher Stowe

Liz Sonneborn

CHELSEA HOUSE
PUBLISHERS
An imprint of Infobase Publishing

HARRIET BEECHER STOWE

Chelsea House
An imprint of Infobase Publishing
132 West 31st Street
New York NY 10001

Library of Congress Cataloging-in-Publication Data
Sonneborn, Liz.
Harriet Beecher Stowe / Liz Sonneborn.
    p. cm. — (Leaders of the Civil War era)
Includes bibliographical references and index.
ISBN 978-1-60413-302-8 (hardcover : acid free paper)
1. Stowe, Harriet Beecher, 1811-1896—Juvenile literature. 2. Stowe, Harriet Beecher, 1811-1896. Uncle Tom's cabin—Juvenile literature. 3. Authors, American—19th century—Biography—Juvenile literature. 4. Abolitionists—United States—Biography—Juvenile literature. 5. United States—History—Civil War, 1861-1865—Literature and the war—Juvenile literature. I. Title. II. Series.
PS2956.S66 2009
813'.3—dc22
[B]   2008044608

Chelsea House books are available at special discounts when purchased in bulk quantities for businesses, associations, institutions, or sales promotions. Please call our Special Sales Department in New York at (212) 967-8800 or (800) 322-8755.

You can find Chelsea House on the World Wide Web at http://www.chelseahouse.com

Series design by Erik Lindstrom
Cover design by Keith Trego

Printed in the United States of America

Bang KT 10 9 8 7 6 5 4 3 2 1

This book is printed on acid-free paper.

All links and Web addresses were checked and verified to be correct at the time of publication. Because of the dynamic nature of the Web, some addresses and links may have changed since publication and may no longer be valid.

CONTENTS

The Book That Changed a Nation

A runaway slave named Eliza races toward the Ohio River, with her young son wrapped in her arms. Behind her is a slave trader, coming "after her like a hound after a deer." "Nerved with strength such as God only gives to the desperate," Eliza reaches the water's edge and leaps onto a chunk of ice in the turgid river. Her bare feet bleeding, she jumps from ice floe to ice floe, determined to carry her child across the river to safety.

A little girl named Eva lies dying in her bed. She is surrounded by her relatives and her family's slaves. All are weeping, except Eva, who, eager to see Jesus in heaven, is ready for death. In her last moments, her father asks, "O, Eva, tell us what you see! What is it?" With a radiant smile on her face, she utters her last words: "O! love,—joy,—peace!"

A devout Christian slave named Tom refuses to tell his hateful master where two fugitive slaves are hiding. His master threatens to kill Tom. Tom is unconcerned over his own fate, because he knows that after death he will ascend to heaven. Yet, he begs his master not to bring "this great sin on your soul!" "Do the worst you can, my troubles'll be over soon," Tom says, "but, if ye don't repent, yours won't *never* end!" Awed by Tom's words, his owner pauses for a moment. Then, once again overtaken by evil and "foaming with rage," he suddenly "[smites] his victim to the ground."

A NOVEL OF SLAVERY

In the late nineteenth century, these three scenes were familiar to virtually every American—man and woman, young and old, rich and poor. They were dramatic episodes from *Uncle Tom's Cabin, or Life Among the Lowly*, a novel published in book form in 1852. During that century, in the United States, the novel sold more copies than any other book except the Bible. It was an international sensation as well, selling huge numbers in countries throughout the world. *Uncle Tom's Cabin* also made its author, Harriet Beecher Stowe, famous. With its publication, Stowe went from being a professor's wife and a mother of six children to being one of the most celebrated women of her time.

What made Stowe's novel so popular? The most obvious reason is that it told a good story and told it well. Stowe created

(Opposite Page) Uncle Tom's Cabin was first published as a 40-week serial in the abolitionist newspaper *National Era* on June 5, 1851. Stowe's story, centering on a long-suffering slave, quickly became popular with readers. On March 20, 1852, her story was published in book form. The book eventually became the best-selling novel in the world in the nineteenth century, and was translated into every major language.

UNCLE TOM'S CABIN;

OR,

LIFE AMONG THE LOWLY.

BY

HARRIET BEECHER STOWE.

VOL. I.

ONE HUNDREDTH THOUSAND.

BOSTON:

JOHN P. JEWETT & COMPANY

CLEVELAND, OHIO:

JEWETT, PROCTOR & WORTHINGTON.

1852.

an array of exciting episodes and interesting characters, who, at least to nineteenth-century audiences, seemed very true to life. She also wrote in a conversational style that rendered her story accessible to readers from all backgrounds. Her intimate tone often made readers feel as though she was talking directly to them.

Given Stowe's gifts as a writer, it was expected that people would be drawn to her prose. What was surprising was how readers were compelled by her subject matter. *Uncle Tom's Cabin* was a novel with a message. From many different angles, it explored slavery as practiced in the mid-nineteenth-century American South, concluding that the institution was a moral blight on the nation. With its controversial subject matter, no one, least of all Stowe herself, expected it to become an epic best-seller.

AWAKENING AMERICA'S CONSCIENCE

The difficult subject, however, only contributed to the novel's success. Through the book, Stowe gave Americans, especially in the North, a way of grappling with the long-festering issue of slavery. Relatives, friends, and neighbors shared their impressions of Stowe's tale, prompting many, perhaps for the first time, to examine the impact slavery was having not only on their country, but also on their own lives.

Stowe encouraged self-examination by making her characters seem familiar to her audience. In Eliza's plight, readers saw their own willingness to do anything to keep their children safe from harm. In Little Eva's death, they were reminded of the beloved babies and children they saw die from disease, a common occurrence at the time. And in Tom's piety, they recognized their own desire to live a life guided by Christ's teachings.

Just as importantly, the stories of these and Stowe's many other characters appealed to the emotions of her readers, freeing them to contemplate slavery in new ways. For decades, anti-slavery advocates had presented the public with newspapers and pamphlets, detailing in words and pictures the horrors of slavery. But Stowe's story was able to reach many people who had previously been indifferent to these tracts. By design, she engaged not just her readers' heads, but their hearts as well. Her prose showed white Americans how to identify and sympathize with African-American slaves, whom many considered less than human before reading Stowe's book.

Ten years after Stowe started writing *Uncle Tom's Cabin*, the tensions between the North and the South ignited into the Civil War (1861–1865). In 1862, the second year of the conflict, President Abraham Lincoln invited Stowe to the White House. When the president met the famous author, he supposedly declared, "So you're the little woman who wrote the book that started this great war!" Although Lincoln most likely never spoke these words, the greeting has become legend, probably because it recognized the enormous impact of Stowe's novel. It may be too much to say that *Uncle Tom's Cabin* was responsible for the Civil War, but it is true that the novel did something few books have ever done. It awoke the conscience of a nation and, in doing so, changed the course of history.

Becoming a
Literary Woman

On June 14, 1811, in the tidy New England town of Litch-field, Connecticut, Roxana Beecher gave birth to a baby girl. She called the infant Harriet after her favorite sister. The name was also a tribute to another of her daughters—a baby, also named Harriet, who had died of whooping cough three years earlier.

Harriet's father was Lyman Beecher, a well-regarded minister in the Congregationalist church. Lyman spent much of his time attending to his parishioners, leaving Roxana in charge of their growing household. Harriet had five older brothers and sisters—Catharine, William, Edward, Mary, and George. In addition, Roxana gave birth to two more boys, Henry and Charles, while Harriet was still a toddler. Because Lyman made little money from his ministry, the family had to take in paying boarders to supplement its income. Caring for her children,

Lyman Beecher *(seated, center)* was one of the most eloquent preachers of his time. He was also a leader in the American religious movement known as the Second Great Awakening. Pictured are 9 of his 14 children. Standing: Thomas, William, Edward, Charles, Henry Ward. Seated: Isabella, Catharine, Mary, and Harriet.

the boarders, and a constant stream of visitors was a strain on Roxana, emotionally and physically. When Harriet was only five, Roxana died of tuberculosis at the age of 41.

Harriet had few vivid memories of Roxana, although she did recall her mother once reading aloud to her from a children's book. Even so, after death, Roxana remained a strong presence in the Beecher household. As Harriet recalled in her contribution to *The Autobiography of Lyman Beecher*, "In every scene of family joy or sorrow, or when father wished to make an appeal to our hearts which he knew we could not resist, he spoke of mother." The Beechers always remembered Roxana as kind and warm, gentle and patient. Throughout her life, Harriet retained this almost saintly view of Roxana as a womanly ideal that she strove to live up to.

GROWING UP IN NEW ENGLAND

After Roxana's sudden death, Lyman Beecher decided to send his youngest daughter for an extended visit with her mother's relatives. For about a year, little Harriet lived with her maternal grandmother and her aunt Harriet in their sprawling home in Guilford, Connecticut. Unlike her quiet mother, her grandmother and aunt were independent and opinionated women. Harriet especially enjoyed spending time with her boisterous aunt. Aunt Harriet was a skilled storyteller, known for her harsh wit and gift for making fun of other people's foibles. Harriet Beecher remembered her childhood visits to Guilford as some of the happiest times of her youth.

By the time Harriet returned to Litchfield, Lyman Beecher had found a new wife (also named Harriet). Her stepmother soon had her own young children to take care of, and Harriet's older siblings were too involved with their schooling to pay much attention to their little sister. Harriet was well dressed and well fed, but she was otherwise largely ignored while growing up in her bustling house.

When Harriet became lonely and desperate for conversation, she headed for the kitchen. There, Harriet enjoyed talking with the servants who prepared meals for the Beechers and their boarders. Years later, she wrote of her fondness for an African-American servant named Candace. During a family prayer service after Roxana's death, Candace saw Harriet's confusion and sorrow. She pulled the little girl into the kitchen and held her until the service was over. "[S]he kissed my hand," Harriet recalled in *The Autobiography of Lyman Beecher*, "and I felt her tears drop upon it. There was something about her feeling that struck me with awe. She scarcely spoke a word, but gave me to understand that she was paying that homage to my mother's memory."

Aside from the kitchen, Harriet's favorite room was her father's study. She liked flipping through Lyman's books as he sat at his desk, working on his Sunday sermons. Many of the books were scholarly works on religion, but there were a few that excited the girl's imagination. She particularly liked the exotic stories in Lyman's volume of *Arabian Nights*.

Lyman frowned on reading fiction, which, due to his strict religious beliefs, he considered a worthless way to spend one's time. When Roxana's relatives came to visit, however, they always brought a stack of novels and poetry collections. Ignoring their father's protests, the Beecher children devoured these books. Harriet was especially a fan of the adventure novels of Sir Walter Scott and the narrative poetry of Lord Byron.

Lyman was far more enthusiastic about his children's interest in debating. He taught his boys how to construct a coherent argument. He then tested their skills by taking one side of an issue and having one of the boys take the other. Harriet was not allowed to take part in these lively household debates because she was a girl. Even so, she eagerly watched and listened, soaking up the same lessons her brothers were taught.

A NINETEENTH-CENTURY GIRLHOOD

In the early nineteenth century, women and men lived in different realms. Men were the breadwinners, while women were largely confined to the home. Of course, at that time, the tasks involved in running a household were extensive, challenging, and often exhausting. Wives were expected to cook, clean, weave cloth, make many household goods (including clothing), and raise large families. While performing all of this difficult work, many women spent most of their adult lives either pregnant or recovering from pregnancies.

Harriet grew up learning about the domestic tasks that then defined a woman's role in society. But she was often envious of her brothers as they prepared to make their way in the wider world. Even Lyman recognized that Harriet had a cleverness and determination that made her more suited for the masculine sphere. As he wrote his brother-in-law in 1819, "Harriet is a great genius—I would give a hundred dollars if she was a boy. . . . She is as odd—as she is intelligent & studious."

Unlike most fathers of the time, Lyman Beecher wanted his girls to get a good education. Luckily for the Beecher sisters, they lived down the street from Litchfield Female Academy. Founded in 1792, it was one of the first schools for girls established in the United States. In colonial America, few saw the need for educating women because they rarely worked outside the home. But after the founding of the United States, some Americans began to argue that for democracy to work, boys needed to be trained to become thinking, dedicated citizens. Because these boys' first teachers were their mothers, it followed that women needed at least a rudimentary education.

Initially, Litchfield offered academic courses in grammar and arithmetic, while emphasizing lessons in painting, embroidery, and other artistic pursuits that proper young ladies were supposed to master. However, by the time Harriet, at age eight, began attending the school, more challenging subjects such as science, philosophy, and Latin had been added to the curriculum. In fact, Litchfield was one of the few American schools where a girl could get as good an academic education as a boy.

Harriet was generally a good student, at least in subjects that interested her. Her favorite was composition, in which students were taught to write about a variety of challenging subjects. At 13, Harriet won a school prize for one of her essays. When it was read out loud at a town exposition, Lyman was impressed enough to ask about its author. Harriet later said that watching his reaction to the news that she had written the piece was the proudest moment of her life.

STUDYING IN HARTFORD

The same year, Harriet left home to attend the Hartford Female Seminary in Hartford, Connecticut, founded by her sister Catharine. Catharine had been engaged to be married

Before the 1800s, women rarely continued their education after grammar school. In the early nineteenth century, secondary schools called academies experienced rapid growth. Some offered women an education equal to that of men. The community in which Harriet Beecher was raised was considered one of the most intellectual in New England.

when her fiancé suddenly died. While grieving, she struggled to figure out what she was going to do with the rest of her life. Catharine became upset when she realized that, even with her Litchfield education, she was not trained to do anything outside the home. She was just as angry over Harriet's limited education. As Catharine wrote to her father in 1823, "I feel anxious that Harriets mind should not be left to run to waste as mine has & should feel a pleasure in taking care of her education."

With Lyman's blessing, Catharine decided to start a school. Because there were no schools for female teachers, she had to train herself. As the school grew, Catharine needed more teachers, so she started a system of hiring promising students as assistant instructors and training them on the job to become full-fledged teachers.

Harriet thrived at Hartford. She enjoyed the all-girl atmosphere in which students studied and lived together, often forming close bonds they would treasure for the rest of their lives. Under Catharine's watchful care, Harriet learned Latin and edited the school's newspaper during her three years at Hartford.

TEACHING SCHOOL

When she graduated, Harriet headed to Boston, Massachusetts, where Lyman and her stepmother were living. Being once again under her father's roof was depressing for Harriet. Her older brothers were all off studying or beginning their careers, and Catharine and her other sister Mary were consumed by their work at the Hartford school. In contrast, Harriet had little to do and even less to look forward to. She wrote to Catharine about her desperation: "I don't know as I am fit for anything, and I have thought that I could wish to die young, and let the remembrance of me and my faults perish in the grave, rather than live, as I fear to do, a trouble to everyone."

Alarmed by Harriet's letter, Catharine came up with a plan. She wrote to Lyman, asking him to allow Harriet to come back to Hartford and train to become a drawing teacher. Catharine correctly guessed that having friends around and meaningful work to do would be the perfect cure for her little sister's depression: "Harriet will have young society here all the time, which she cannot have at home, and I think cheerful and amusing friends will do much for her. I can do better in preparing her to teach drawing than any one else, for I best know what is needed."

Once back at Hartford, Harriet worked hard in her new position. She wrote her grandmother that she was "employed from nine in the morning till after dark at night," adding, "I am very comfortable and happy." Harriet diligently studied drawing, but she found her true calling in teaching composition. For a time, she also became the school's unofficial principal when Catharine, overwhelmed by her responsibilities, had a near breakdown and left the school to recover. Catharine instructed all the teachers to work together to run the school, but, somewhat to Harriet's surprise, she naturally emerged as Hartford's leader. The experience gave Harriet a new sense of confidence. In a letter home, she wrote, "I shall speak in the Hall again Monday. I now feel as if I could do anything."

Although the Hartford school attracted students from across the country, Catharine never found a way to make it financially successful. When in 1832 Lyman announced he was considering a post as the head of the Lane Theological Seminary in Cincinnati, Ohio, Catharine decided to go with him and start fresh. Hartford stayed open for a time, but from then on it was run by male teachers. No longer a school for women run by women, it lost much of the welcoming ambience that Harriet had enjoyed as a student there.

HEADING WEST

With Catharine and three of her brothers, Harriet headed out to Cincinnati. To the Beecher clan, moving west was not just a change of scenery; it was a change in their way of life. The Beechers were steeped in the culture of New England, where society was ruled by time-honored manners and traditions. Cincinnati, then considered part of the American West, was a freer and looser place, not subject to the sometimes-stifling social rules of the East. That was exactly what attracted Lyman to the city. He felt the West was too wild and needed to be tamed by old-fashioned New England values.

While Lyman went to the West to change it, his children had a different goal. They went to Cincinnati with a sense of adventure, ready to revel in the city's open-minded society. Harriet's little brother Henry, then a student at Amherst College, wrote her about his enthusiastic response on hearing of Lyman's plans: "I fairly *danced.* . . . I sang, whistled, flew around like a mad man[,] Father's removal to the West is my 'hearts desire.'"

By the time the Beechers arrived, Cincinnati was a boomtown. Located on the Ohio River, it was the most important commercial center in the western United States. Harriet was awed by the traffic of steamships that carried goods in and out of the growing city.

During her first years in Cincinnati, Harriet taught at Catharine's new school, the Western Female Institute. But, for

WITNESSING SLAVERY

Before moving to Cincinnati, Ohio, Harriet Beecher had never had any direct experience with the institution of slavery. In her home state of Connecticut, slavery was not legal. Growing up she had known a few African Americans, but they were hired servants, not slaves.

Ohio was also a free state. But in Kentucky, just across the Ohio River, slavery was permitted. In 1833, Beecher paid a visit to a Kentucky plantation. She was accompanied by Mary Dutton, who, like Beecher, was a teacher at the Western Female Institute. Many years later, Dutton shared her memories of the excursion with Beecher's son Charles, who included Dutton's account in his *Life of Harriet Beecher Stowe* (1889): "Harriet did not seem to notice

Harriet, teaching had lost its luster. She had become far more interested in another career—that of a writer. In 1833, Harriet published her first book, *Primary Geography for Children*. From her own classroom experience, Harriet knew that there was no adequate textbook on American geography. She rightly suspected there would be a good market for such a textbook, because, with the country's changing borders, geography was increasingly considered a necessary part of a good education. Harriet's book was a solid success. She earned about $190 from its publication, which was roughly what Catharine made for a year of teaching.

THE SEMI-COLON CLUB

After the publication of *Primary Geography*, Harriet was invited to join the Semi-Colon Club. This social and literary club met

anything in particular that happened, but sat much of the time as though abstracted in thought. When the negroes did funny things and cut up capers, she did not seem to pay the slighted attention to them."

But, in fact, Beecher's initial encounter with Southern slaves had actually left a profound impression on her. The Kentucky plantation she visited later served as the model for the estate of Arthur Shelby, owner of the slave Uncle Tom at the beginning of *Uncle Tom's Cabin*. As Dutton explained, "[I]n reading 'Uncle Tom,' I recognized scene after scene of that visit portrayed with the most minute fidelity, and knew at once where the material for that portion of the story had been gathered."

at the house of Samuel Foote, Harriet's maternal uncle, who had moved to Cincinnati years before. The elite of Cincinnati society, the "Semi-Colons" gathered every Monday evening. At each session, one man would read aloud stories and essays written by the group. Everyone would then discuss the pieces, offering both praise and criticism. After the readings, the Semi-Colons enjoyed refreshments and dancing.

For Harriet, attending the Semi-Colon Club seemed exciting and even a little dangerous. At first, she refused to sign her work, being too scared of criticism to admit it was hers. But when the Semi-Colons consistently praised her efforts, her confidence grew. She wrote more and more, experimenting with different styles and forms, working diligently to develop her own voice.

Harriet Beecher's hard work paid off. Her work caught the attention of James Hall, one of the Semi-Colons who published *Western Literary Magazine*. In a letter to her brother George, Harriet described what was for her a particularly gratifying session of the Semi-Colon Club: "I wrote a piece, a little bit of a love sketch & sent it in—thinking it was rather a contemptible little affair—& indeed much hesitating whether I would have it read at all—But somehow or other every body was mightily taken with it—& I have heard more about it since than anything I ever did—Judge Hall wants to put it in his magazine & so I have promised it to him & so you will see it."

The story was the first of many Harriet Beecher would publish in national magazines. After years of playing the dutiful daughter, the diligent student, and the dedicated teacher, she had finally found her own place in the world. From then on, Beecher would be what Americans of the day called a "literary woman."

Housekeeping and Writing

The Semi-Colon Club not only bolstered Harriet Beecher's confidence as a writer, it also introduced her to a circle of intellectual friends who shared her interests. Even more importantly, in a time when men and women lived much of their lives in separate spheres, the club gave her an opportunity to get to know some of the most eligible bachelors in Cincinnati. The married people in the group often gossiped about the singles, actively trying to pair up young men and women who they believed would make a good match.

Beecher disliked their meddling, but she was even more unnerved by her relatives' speculations about her romantic life. Her father, Lyman, was fairly convinced that, like her older sister Catharine, Harriet would never marry. In an era when nearly every woman became a wife and a mother, Beecher did seem well positioned to remain unwed. Unlike most American women of her time, she had a good education, and through her writing and her teaching, she had already proved her ability to earn a living from her own labor.

A PARTNER FOR LIFE

During the summer of 1834, Harriet Beecher took a trip east to see her brother Henry graduate from Amherst. It turned out to be a good time to be away from Cincinnati. The city was an important center for hog slaughtering, and the blood and waste of the animals mixed with the city's water supply, making Cincinnati a hotbed of epidemic disease, especially in the warmer months. That summer, a terrible epidemic of cholera swept through the city. One of its victims was Eliza Stowe, a vivacious young woman who Harriet counted as one of her closest friends among the Semi-Colons.

When Beecher returned to Cincinnati, she immediately called on Calvin Stowe, Eliza's grieving husband. A Massachusetts native, Stowe had grown up poor, but with the financial help of local ministers, he had attended Bowdoin College and the Andover Theological Seminary. Before graduating, he had mastered French, Spanish, German, Hebrew, Greek, and Arabic. Stowe came to Cincinnati to take a teaching post at the Lane Theological Seminary, of which Lyman Beecher was the president. By that time, Stowe was known as one of the leading Biblical scholars in the United States.

Prone to gloominess, Calvin Stowe was devastated by his wife's sudden death. He was greatly comforted by visits from Beecher, who, as a minister's daughter, was experienced in caring for those who had lost a loved one. In a letter, Stowe told her that whenever he was overwhelmed with grief he thought of her: "I thank God that he has given me a female friend to whom I can open my heart."

Less than a year after Eliza Stowe's death, Stowe's friendly feelings for Beecher had turned to love. He wrote to her, declar-

Scholar and educator Calvin Ellis Stowe was very supportive of Harriet's writing. Calvin also was an important school reformer. An enduring result of his work is the system of tax-supported public schools. In 1867, he wrote the best-seller *Origin and History of the Books of the Bible*, one of the first books to examine the Bible from a historical perspective.

ing, "I have a sort of feeling of inseparableness, as though my blood somehow circulated through your veins, and if you were to be torn from me I should *bleed to death*." The couple talked of marriage, but Beecher was hesitant to make that commitment—a sentiment not uncommon in educated young women of the early nineteenth century. After all, marriage would loosen the tight familial bonds she felt with her father, brothers, and sisters. It would also lead to motherhood. Since women then often died in childbirth, coming to terms with marriage also meant coming to terms with the possibility of an early death.

By January 1836, Beecher had overcome her trepidation. She and Stowe were married at home with little fanfare. In fact, the wedding was so low-key that the local papers were confused over whether Harriet or Catharine was the bride. Harriet wrote a witty clarification to her relatives in the East: "[H]e married *me*, & whether he married her too or not is no concern of mine—he doesn't seem to remember whether he did or not."

A NEW TYPE OF MARRIAGE

In nineteenth-century America, husbands were expected to dominate over their submissive wives. But from the beginning, Calvin and Harriet sought a different type of marriage. They saw themselves as intellectual equals and strove for a union based on companionship and mutual respect. As Calvin once wrote Harriet, "I believe there are very few husbands and wives in the world, who have so many real good talks together on such matters as we have."

Yet almost immediately society's separate demands on men and women intruded on the high hopes they had for their married life. Six months after their wedding, Calvin, as the family breadwinner, left their home to travel to Europe, where he was charged with purchasing books for Lane's library. Harriet, now pregnant, was left behind. It was a pattern that would continue throughout their marriage: Often because of Calvin's work and sometimes because of Harriet's, the two would live apart for long stretches.

While away, Calvin relied on Harriet to help his professional career. He had agreed to submit a series of letters about

AMERICAN SLAVERY IN THE EARLY NINETEENTH CENTURY

In 1787, the Constitution of the United States gave each state the right to regulate slavery within its borders. The provision was a concession to states in the South, where the forced labor of African slaves had long been a crucial part of the economy. Over the next few decades, one by one, Northern states (where slavery was less pervasive) moved to abolish the institution, largely on moral grounds. As a result, by the early nineteenth century, the country was divided into slave states, in which slavery was still legal, and free states, in which it was not.

As the United States expanded, tensions between the Southern slave states and Northern free states grew, with both sides jockeying for power. The conflict was evident in the political battle over the proposed statehood for Missouri. Although Missouri applied for admittance into the Union as a slave state, some Northern politicians moved to impose measures on Missouri that would gradually phase out slavery there. The idea outraged many Southern congressmen. After an emotionally charged debate, the matter was finally settled through the Missouri Compromise of 1820. Congress agreed to let Missouri enter the Union as a slave state only on the condition that Maine would be admitted as a free one. Although this conflict was settled peaceably within the halls of Congress, it suggested that the political battle over slavery and its expansion was far from over.

In 1833, the British Parliament passed the Abolition of Slavery Act, which called for the freeing of all British slaves within four years. In the United States, this act helped

(continues)

(continued)
galvanize the growing abolition movement, which called for the end of slavery across America. The most influential American abolitionist was William Lloyd Garrison, who started publishing his antislavery newspaper, *The Liberator*, in 1831. While some American antislavery activists called for a gradual phasing out of slavery, Garrison argued that slavery was a sin and, as such, should be abolished immediately.

While most abolitionists lived in free states, Americans' personal feelings about slavery were not wholly dictated by where they lived. Some Southerners supported the antislavery movement, while some Northerners embraced proslavery sentiments. By the 1830s, slavery was a hot issue across the country, often with neighbors in the same community, or even family members in the same house, holding opposing views.

his travels for publication in the *Cincinnati Journal*. But while traveling, he found himself too busy to write. In order to fulfill his commitment, he turned to Harriet. Calvin wrote to his wife, asking her to craft the pieces for him by extracting from his letters home "all that may [be] suitable and interesting, and fix them up & embellish them in your own way."

During Calvin's absence, Harriet was also caught up in a political controversy that was engulfing Cincinnati. In the summer of 1836, a mob attacked the office of *The Philanthropist*, a prominent antislavery newspaper published by abolitionist James Birney. Although Cincinnati was in a free state, many people in the city were proslavery and were offended by Birney's views. These angry citizens tore the printing press out of his office and tossed it into the Ohio River. Three days of violence followed, until the mayor allowed vigilantes to confront the mob. Stowe's little brother Henry joined the vigilante group, leaving Stowe envious. She said that if she were a man she would happily take a gun down to Birney's office and guard it against attack.

Stowe did take action by writing a letter to the *Cincinnati Journal*, which was then edited by Henry. Her letter condemned the mob for ignoring Birney's property rights and challenging the freedom of the press. The incident also left her sympathetic to the antislavery cause. As she wrote Calvin, "For my part, I can easily see how such proceedings may make converts to abolitionism, for already my sympathies are strongly enlisted for Mr. Birney."

THE STOWE FAMILY GROWS

By the fall of 1836, Stowe's attention turned to matters closer to home. In September, she gave birth to twin girls. At Calvin's insistence, she named them Eliza and Harriet (known to the family as Hatty), in honor of his two wives. Catharine wrote to their relatives, praising Stowe's dedication in caring for her newborns. Jokingly, she said, "Harriet manages better than folk would expect who are wont to think a genius...cannot be good for anything else."

But even after Calvin returned from Europe, his wife struggled to care for her new family. By nature, she was not very skilled at running a household. She tended to focus on one thing and pour her considerable energies into it, however, domestic work in the nineteenth century required women to do many things at once. A woman had to be ready to prepare a meal one moment, then attend to a crying infant the next, all the while making sure her husband had everything he needed.

Calvin was frustrated by Harriet's housekeeping skills. Yet their marriage faced even more serious strains. Calvin had trouble getting the salary from Lane that he had been promised, leaving the couple in constant financial trouble. In addition, the Stowes, although intellectually compatible, had different emotional temperaments. Calvin was prone to emotional outbursts, both of love and anger. Harriet tended to keep her feelings in check and was baffled by Calvin's need to express whatever emotions bubbled up in him.

The stresses of their domestic life only worsened as the size of their family increased. By 1840, Harriet had given birth to two more children—Henry and Frederick (nicknamed Fred). Despite their financial difficulties, Stowe insisted on hiring household servants to help her care for the house and the children. For brief periods, she hired recent European immigrants or black women, some of whom were escaped slaves.

After one black woman had worked for the Stowes for several months, Calvin found out that her former master had arrived in Cincinnati, determined to capture her and take her back to his plantation. Calvin and Henry, who had embraced the abolitionist cause, armed themselves and traveled with the woman along back roads to a station on the Underground Railroad. This network of secret safe houses helped slaves escape to freedom in free states or in Canada.

FINDING TIME TO WRITE

Stowe's most loyal servant was Anna Smith, a young Englishwoman she hired soon after the twins were born. Smith, who came to think of Stowe as a big sister, lived in the Stowe household for the next 18 years. With Smith always there to care for the children, Stowe was able to find time to write, which in turn helped pay for the labor of Smith and her other servants.

During the 1830s and early 1840s, Stowe worked for three different magazines. For *Western Monthly Magazine*, she wrote sketches of prominent westerners, mostly for a male audience. For *Godey's Lady's Book*, the leading women's magazine in the United States, she wrote stories based on her domestic life. For the *New-York Evangelist*, she wrote fiction dealing with religious topics, such as the growing temperance movement, which sought to discourage the consumption and sale of alcohol.

In 1842, Harper Brothers, a publisher in Boston, Massachusetts, contacted Stowe. The firm wanted to print a collection of 15 of her stories. The next year, Harper published *The Mayflower; or, Sketches of Scenes and Characters Among the Descendants of the Pilgrims*. Much of her work was previously credited to Mrs. H. B. Stowe, but at Calvin's suggestion, her name on *The Mayflower* title page appeared as Mrs. Harriet Beecher Stowe. In a letter, Calvin had advised her to "write yourself only and always, *Harriet Beecher Stowe*, which is a name euphonious, flowing, and full of meaning." The pen name was a good marketing tool, given that the names Beecher and Stowe had significance to a good portion of her readership. Calvin Stowe was well regarded as a scholar in religious circles, while Lyman Beecher had become nationally known for a published collection of his sermons on temperance.

YEAR OF STRESS AND STRUGGLE

The publication of *The Mayflower* was, as yet, the high point of Stowe's literary career. However, the rest of the 1840s proved a difficult period for her. Even with household help, the demands of her family were taking a toll on Stowe, both physically and mentally. Nineteenth-century women were expected to be "angels of the house"—kind and loving figures who saw that all their family's needs were met without ever complaining or losing their tempers. The stories of her always calm, always patient mother, Roxana, only reinforced this ideal in Stowe's mind. As a result, when Stowe looked at her own domestic skills, she inevitably found herself wanting. As she wrote to Calvin, "[It] drinks up all my strength to care for & provide for all this family, to try to cure the faults of all—harmonise all—alas it is too much for me & an aching head & heart often show it."

Like many Americans in the 1840s, Stowe was also struggling in her spiritual life. In the West, large religious revivals, associated with the phenomenon now known as the Second Great Awakening, made people rethink their religious beliefs and the place of religion in their everyday lives. Stowe, likewise, reexamined her faith, resulting in a new and nagging determination to become a better Christian. While negotiating with Harper Brothers in Boston, she wrote Calvin of her inner struggle: "Now by the grace of God I am resolved to come home & live for God—It is time to prepare to die . . . Will you dear husband join with me in simplicity & earnestness to lead a new life—& to live no more as we have—allowing ourselves in sin here & there."

The spiritual stress of the era contributed to a disaster within the Beecher family. Stowe's brother George, a minister who was in the midst of a personal religious crisis, shot himself in the head in the summer of 1843. The suicide shocked Stowe, making her only more concerned about her faith. Writing to her siblings, she asked, "[D]ear brothers, sisters, who is to be called next?—Are we ready—Have we put on the Lord Jesus?"

Weeks after George's death, Stowe gave birth to another girl, whom she named Georgiana. Ill from a difficult pregnancy, Stowe also faced the day-to-day strain of caring for boarders, who Calvin had insisted they take into their house to help make ends meet. By the summer of 1845, Stowe was heading toward a breakdown. She wrote Calvin of her misery: "It is a dark, sloppy, rainy, muddy, disagreeable day, and I have been working hard (for me) all day in the kitchen, washing dishes . . . I am sick of the smell of sour milk, and sour meat, and sour everything, and then the clothes *will* not dry . . . and everything smells mouldy; and altogether I feel as if I never wanted to eat again."

THE WATER CURE

After surviving a bout of cholera, Stowe insisted to her husband that, for her health, she needed to take break from

Water cure therapy, developed in eighteenth-century Great Britain, became especially popular in the nineteenth century among the wealthy. Varieties of water-related treatment—including drinking and bathing in seawater, and other activities associated with modern-day spas—were believed to cure illness as well as heal and nurture the skin. This picture shows guests at Hathorn Spring in Saratoga, New York, drinking waters which were said to have therapeutic properties.

the pressures of her daily responsibilities. In 1846, Stowe distributed the children among relatives and headed off to Brattleboro, Vermont, to take the water cure. The water cure was a new fad for Americans who felt ill-served by the medical practices of the day. Its regime promised patients that they could live a healthy life without doctors or drugs. The "cure" called for eating moderately, abstaining from alcohol, and exercising in fresh air. It also involved water in just about every way imaginable. In addition to drinking copious amounts, patients at Brattleboro spent much of their time bathing, showering, and soaking in water, or lounging while their entire bodies were wrapped in dripping gauze.

Stowe came to swear by the water cure. As Stowe biographer Joan D. Hedrick points out, the reaction was hardly surprising. As a young woman, Stowe had often been treated with what were known as blue pills. This popular drug of the day contained mercurous chloride. Many of the ailments Stowe had suffered throughout the years, including headaches, fatigue, and mental fogginess, were likely caused by mercury poisoning. Just drinking plenty of water probably helped clear her system of the dangerous blue pills.

Stowe also reveled in the respite from family obligations during her stay at Brattleboro. Instead of caring for her household all day, she could take leisurely hikes, many miles at a time, or just sit and read. More like a contemporary spa than a hospital, Brattleboro also offered amusements that she had not enjoyed since leaving school. Patients spent their evenings playing music or engaging in lively conversations in the parlor. Despite her husband's constant pleading for her to come home, Stowe spent a year relaxing in Vermont.

A PROUD MOTHER

When Stowe came back to Cincinnati, she felt better than she had in years. Nine months later, she gave birth to her sixth child, Samuel Charles. Charley was plump and healthy, and Stowe felt a special affection for the boy. As Calvin wrote her, "[Y]ou are so proud of your baby, one would think you never saw a baby before."

In the summer of 1849, Calvin left the family to take the water cure for himself. While he was away, cholera once again struck Cincinnati. To Stowe's horror, Charley, then only about a year and a half old, came down with the disease. Perhaps because he had been in such good health, Charley suffered for many days before succumbing. The image of Charley's pain in his final hours would be vivid in Stowe's mind for the rest of her life.

Scarred by this last experience with cholera, the Stowes decided to leave Cincinnati. Calvin accepted a post at Bowdoin College in Brunswick, Maine. After 18 years, Harriet Beecher Stowe was ready to give up on her western adventure and start a new life in the familiar eastern landscape of her youth.

Finding a Cause

In the spring of 1850, Stowe left Cincinnati. Her husband, Calvin, stayed behind because he needed to fulfill old teaching commitments at the Lane Theological Seminary before he could start his new job at Bowdoin College in Maine. Both agreed that Harriet should go on ahead without him so she could establish a new family home in the East.

Stowe did not go directly to Maine, however. During her trip, she took the opportunity to visit a few of her siblings along the way. She stopped by Brooklyn, New York, to see her brother Henry, who was now the minister of the city's famous Plymouth Church. Stowe then headed to Hartford, Connecticut, to visit with her sister Mary. Next, she traveled on to Boston, Massachusetts, the hometown of her brother Edward and his wife, Isabella.

THE FUGITIVE SLAVE LAW

At each stop, Stowe talked with her siblings about a possible new law that was being discussed in the U.S. Congress. Called the Fugitive Slave Act, it set out legal mechanisms by which slave owners could retrieve runaway slaves who had escaped to free states in the North. Since 1793, there had been a law on the books concerning the return of fugitive slaves, but it had been largely ignored. Southerners in Congress made it clear that they wanted the new law enforced.

The Fugitive Slave Act of 1850 required citizens to "aid and assist in the prompt and efficient execution of this law, whenever their services may be required." As a result, Americans, even those in free states, could be fined $1,000 and jailed for six months if they gave shelter, food, or other assistance to an escaping slave. The law set out new rules for dealing with a slave owner's claim that a seemingly free African American was actually a runaway slave who belonged to him. Such cases would now be settled by a federal commissioner. If this official decided the African American was in fact a runaway, he received $10. But if the commissioner decided the owner was lying and the African American was actually a free black, he received only $5. Clearly, the law rewarded unscrupulous commissioners who decided cases in favor of the slave owner, no matter what the facts suggested. In addition, African Americans found to be slaves had no legal recourse. They were not permitted to request an appeal of a commissioner's decision in court.

Stowe's siblings were appalled by the Fugitive Slave Act, which was adopted in September 1850. Especially outraged were Edward and his wife, Isabella, who had both become fierce abolitionists. After Stowe had settled in Maine, they wrote letters to her about the terrible abuses of the law occurring in Boston. Routinely, free blacks were captured by Southerners falsely claiming to be their owners. Edward and Isabella were

As depicted in this painting, under the Fugitive Slave Act, escaped slaves were returned to their masters and private citizens were obligated to assist in their recapture. Abolitionists, appalled by the passage of this law, increased in numbers; the Underground Railroad became more efficient; and new Personal Liberty Laws were passed in many anti-slavery states. The last chapter of *Uncle Tom's Cabin* urged white Northerners to welcome escaped slaves and to treat them with respect.

infuriated by these injustices. They were equally disgusted that, because of the law, they were now expected to participate in the return of runaways. Northerners could no longer feel untainted by the sin of slavery.

EMBRACING THE ANTISLAVERY MOVEMENT

As soon as Stowe arrived in Maine, she remembered how much she had missed New England. Quickly getting to know some of the Bowdoin professors and their wives, she found a new and exciting circle of friends. In July 1850, in her comfortable home in the town of Brunswick, Stowe gave birth to her last child, which also helped relieve her grief over losing her beloved Charley a year earlier. She called the infant Charles Edward as a tribute to her dead son.

As her raw grief subsided, it was replaced by anger over the injustice of the boy's early death. She began to channel this anger toward the antislavery cause, as she received letter after letter from relatives about the horrible treatment of African Americans, both enslaved and free. Catharine Beecher was delighted by Stowe's newfound passion. As she wrote her little sister, "Your last letter was a real good one, it did my heart good to find somebody in as indignant a state as I am about this miserable wicked fugitive slave business—Why I have felt almost choked sometimes with pent up wrath that does no good."

For Stowe, that "pent up wrath" was profoundly frustrating. She did not want to just write letters about the moral horror of slavery to her brothers and sisters. She wanted to *do* something about it. In the nineteenth century, however, women were barred from the political arena. Not only were they denied the vote, they were also discouraged from even discussing politics, because it was not considered a proper subject for well-bred women to contemplate.

Within her family and among her sophisticated friends, Stowe felt comfortable expressing antislavery views, but that provided little comfort. She found herself jealous of her little brother Henry, who, as a nationally famous minister, could reach a wide audience with his sermons. She wrote to him to encourage his work, while at the same time bemoaning her own inability to make a difference: "Must we [women] forever keep calm and smile and smile when every sentiment of manliness and humanity is kicked and rolled in the dust and lies trampled and bleeding and make it a merit to be exceedingly cool—I feel as if my heart would burn itself out in grief and shame that such things are—I wish I had your chance—but next best to that is to have you have it—so fire away—give them no rest day or night."

WRITING TO MAKE A CHANGE

Stowe, however, did have an outlet to express herself that was unavailable to most other women of her day—her writing. In the five years before moving to Maine, Stowe had written little. She was, therefore, a bit surprised and a great deal flattered when Sarah Josepha Hale, the editor of *Godey's Lady's Book*, asked to include a sketch about her in a book of biographies of 2,500 women throughout history. So long consumed by the responsibilities of a wife and a mother, Stowe was pleased by this reminder that she was also a writer.

Just as Stowe was thinking of reviving her literary career, Gamaliel Bailey contacted her. Bailey was the editor of the *National Era*, a weekly newspaper with a circulation of about 15,000. Read by both men and women, the periodical printed stories and poetry with political commentary mixed in. The *National Era* took an antislavery stance, but its writing was less fiery than the famous antislavery newspaper *The Liberator*. With Bailey's encouragement, Stowe wrote a story for the *National Era*'s August 1850 issue. Titled "The Freeman's Dream," it was a fable of the evils of the Fugitive Slave Law. The story told of an escaped slave who asked a farmer for food. Knowing about the law, the farmer refused and the slave was captured by his former owner. Consumed by guilt, the farmer then had a dream that reminded him that God's law is greater than any made by man. In the dream, he died and rose to heaven, where he was judged as a sinner for refusing to feed the hungry.

In the first weeks of 1851, Henry Ward Beecher paid his sister a visit. Arriving at about midnight, Henry stayed up talking with Harriet until dawn. The two excitedly shared their views

Henry Ward Beecher was against slavery and bigotry of any kind, and he believed that Christianity should adapt with the changing of the times. He raised funds to buy weapons for those willing to oppose slavery in Kansas and Nebraska, and his church supported a volunteer infantry regiment during the American Civil War. Here he is pictured with his sister Harriet.

about abolition and what they wanted to do to fight slavery. Years later, in a letter to her friend George Eliot, Stowe recalled their conversation: "Henry told me then that he meant to fight that battle in New York, that he would have a church that would stand by him to resist the tyranic dictation of Southern slave-holders. . . . I said: I, too, have begun to do something; I have begun a story, trying to set forth sufferings and wrongs of the slaves." That night, brother and sister pledged to support each other in serving the abolitionist struggle—him from the pulpit, her from the page.

Stowe was also encouraged to write about slavery by her sister-in-law Isabella. In a letter, Isabella wrote, "Now, Hattie, if I could use a pen as you can, I would write something that would make this whole nation feel what an accursed thing slavery is." Stowe's son Charles, who at this time was still a baby, later explained his mother's reaction to Isabella's words in his book, *Life of Harriet Beecher Stowe* (1889). According to Charles, when Isabella's letter was read out loud in the family parlor, Stowe "rose up from her chair" and declared "I will write something, I will if I live."

THE ORIGINS OF *UNCLE TOM'S CABIN*

Stowe herself had several versions of the story of how she began writing *Uncle Tom's Cabin*. Years later, she claimed that the germ of the book came to her in church one Sunday in February 1851. There, Stowe said she had a vision of a slave being brutally beaten. When she got home, she quickly wrote out the death scene of a character she called Uncle Tom. With Calvin out of town, she sat her sons Henry and Fred down and read to them what she had written. When they both broke out in tears, she knew she had a story to tell.

A friend of Stowe's later told the editor of *The Life and Letters of Harriet Beecher Stowe* (1897) another version of the novel's origin. She said that Stowe told her it all began during a visit to the Andover Theological Seminary, where Calvin had accepted a job. After lunch, the couple stopped off at their lodgings to take a nap. As Calvin fell asleep, Stowe was overtaken with inspiration. Without stopping, she quickly wrote out nine pages recounting Tom's death scene. When Calvin woke up, she said, "I want you to listen to this and see if it will do." As she read the fresh pages, he began to weep. When she finished, he shouted, "Do! I should think it would do!"

However, as she wrote to Bailey in March 1851, Stowe actually began her first novel as a new multipart story for the *National Era*. She explained that until recently she had not felt compelled to write much about slavery, but lately she felt an urgency to do so: "But I feel now that the time is come when even a woman or a child who can speak a word for freedom and humanity is bound to speak." She planned to "show the *best side* of the thing, and something *faintly approaching the worst*," using words to paint mental pictures in her readers' minds. "There is no arguing with *pictures*," she explained, "and everybody is impressed by them, whether they mean to be or not." Stowe estimated that her story could run in serial installments over about three or four issues.

RESEARCHING THE NOVEL

As Stowe got deeper into the writing process, she quickly discovered two things. The first was that she needed far more space to tell her story. Her series would eventually expand from three to four installments to 44 chapters, one of which ran in nearly every issue of the *National Era* appearing between June 1851 and April 1852. The second was that she would need to perform additional research if she was to depict slavery realistically and truthfully.

As Stowe noted in her letter to Bailey, she initially felt she would not have to do any research at all. Her story, she explained, would involve "incidents which have occurred in the sphere of my observation, incidents which have occurred in the sphere of my personal knowledge, or in the knowledge of

Josiah Henson, born a slave in Maryland, escaped to Ontario, Canada, in 1830, where he later founded a settlement and a school for other fugitive slaves. Henson's autobiography, *The Life of Josiah Henson*, was said to be an inspiration for the main character in *Uncle Tom's Cabin*.

my friends." But Stowe's direct knowledge of slavery was slight. It was largely limited to one brief visit to a Kentucky plantation in 1833 and her conversations with black domestic servants she had hired over the years. As she confidently wrote to her

THE PLOT OF *UNCLE TOM'S CABIN*

The novel *Uncle Tom's Cabin* tells two stories with African-American heroes—one about Uncle Tom, who suffers horribly under slavery, and one about the Harris family, who free themselves from the cruel institution by escaping first to Canada and eventually to Africa. Both stories begin at a Kentucky plantation owned by Arthur Shelby. Struggling with debt, Shelby (over the objections of his wife Emily) decides to sell two of his slaves—Uncle Tom and Harry, the young son of Emily's maid, Eliza Harris.

Tom does not resist, but Eliza decides to flee north with Harry. (Her husband, George, has already run away, promising his wife to some day buy her and Harry's freedom.) Chased by Harry's new owner, Haley, Eliza makes a harrowing escape, jumping from ice floe to ice floe to cross the Ohio River. Eliza is taken in by the family of Ohio senator Bird, whose wife convinces him to help the runaways in violation of the Fugitive Slave Law. With the Birds' assistance, Eliza and Harry find refuge in a Quaker settlement, where they are reunited with George.

Meanwhile, Haley puts Tom on a riverboat bound for Louisiana. While aboard, Tom saves a little girl named Eva, who has fallen overboard. At Eva's request, her father, Augustine St. Clare, buys Tom and takes him to the St. Clare home in New Orleans. Tom is treated well by the St. Clares. He and Eva form a tight bond as she reads the Bible to him. Also in the St. Clare household is Ophelia, Augustine's sister, who is charged with educating Topsy, a mischievous slave girl.

The physically fragile little Eva grows ill. In her final days, she makes her father promise to free Tom. But before St. Clare can do so, he is accidentally killed. His cruel wife

(continues)

(continued)

ignores Eva's wishes and auctions off Tom. His new owner
is Simon Legree, a northerner who treats the slaves on his
Southern plantation brutally. He has special contempt for
Tom because of his intense Christian piety.

Cassy, Legree's slave mistress, wants to kill Legree but
Tom prevents her. She and another slave named Emmeline
then hide in the attic as they plot their escape. When Tom
refuses to tell Legree where they are, Legree beats him. As
Tom lays dying, George Shelby, the son of his former master,
finds him. George had hoped to buy Tom and set him free,
but instead Tom dies in his arms.

Cassy and Emmeline escape to a ship bound for the
North. On board, it is revealed that Cassy is Eliza's mother.
Eventually, she is reunited with the Harrises, who have made
their way to Canada. The family decides to move to Liberia,
an African nation created for ex-slaves. Ophelia takes Topsy to
Vermont for her education. When she grows up, she becomes
a missionary in Africa. George Shelby returns to his father's
plantation and frees his slaves in the name of Uncle Tom.

brother Henry, "I have known a great many slaves—had them
in my family[,] known their history & feelings and seen how
alike their heart beats to any other throbbing heart." It does
not seem to have occurred to her that the employer-employee
relationship she had with black women might have limited her
ability to fully understand these women's intimate lives.

Eventually recognizing that she needed to know more about
the slave experience, Stowe started reading press accounts and
books about slavery as she began to craft her tale. She was
particularly drawn to the popular genre of the slave narrative.

These exciting tales described slaves' escapes to freedom in their own words. She was especially influenced by the narratives of Josiah Henson and Henry Bibb, both of whom passed through Cincinnati as they fled north.

As her story grew longer, she saw that she also needed more firsthand information about Southern plantation life. She wrote to Frederick Douglass, the most prominent African-American antislavery activist of the era, pleading for his help. She explained that she had located "an able paper written by a Southern planter," but felt the perspective was incomplete. She asked Douglass if he could help her get in touch with an ex-slave who could describe a plantation from the slave's point of view. Desperate for information about slave auctions, she also enlisted the help of her brother Charles. Then a minister in Newark, New Jersey, he had worked in New Orleans 10 years earlier and had witnessed the buying and selling of slaves there. At Stowe's request, he came for a visit just to tell Stowe everything he remembered about his experiences down South. His description of a vicious overseer provided the model for her novel's great villain, Simon Legree.

HELP AT HOME

In a different way, Catharine Beecher was even more supportive of Stowe's work. She moved into the Stowe household to take care of the children while Stowe completed her novel. After breakfast every morning, Catharine insisted that Harriet leave the house and work with Calvin in his quiet office. Catharine wrote to her sister Mary, "There was no other way to keep her out of the family cares & quietly at work & since this plan is adopted she goes ahead finely."

Even with Catharine's help, Stowe struggled to meet her deadlines. Week after week, she had to file new installments with Bailey. It was a grueling schedule, but Stowe always had Bailey's support. He saw his readership grow weekly and wanted to do anything he could to keep Stowe writing the popular story. As pressure-filled as the assignment was, Stowe also benefited from having to write so quickly. Readers sent in enthusiastic fan letters, which kept her excited about the difficult project. Stowe could see that her serial was striking a chord with the *National Era*'s readership. Yet she could never have suspected the tremendous impact her story was about to have on American culture and history.

A National
Sensation

Even before she had completed the serial, Stowe began searching for a publisher for *Uncle Tom's Cabin*. With her sister Catharine's help, she first approached Phillips, Sampson, and Company, which had published several books by Catharine. The company turned down Stowe's novel, probably fearing that *Uncle Tom's Cabin* would be unpopular with Southern readers. Most likely, the publisher also doubted that a book by a woman on such a controversial subject as slavery would sell well anywhere.

Luckily for Stowe, John P. Jewett, owner of a small religious publishing company based in Boston, Massachusetts, saw some real promise in *Uncle Tom's Cabin*. His wife had read out loud to him the chapter recounting the death of Little Eva, a favorite character of fans of the *National Era* serial. At her insistence,

Jewett decided to offer Stowe a book contract. In his initial meeting with the Stowes, Jewett suggested that they put up half the publication costs and then he and the Stowes would split all profits 50-50. Calvin Stowe demurred. As usual, the family was strapped for cash, and he felt they could not risk paying half the production budget. Jewett then agreed to pay for the production and proposed two different deals: He could give the Stowes 20 percent of the profits or he could give the Stowes 10 percent and sink the other 10 percent into promoting the book. Calvin agreed to the latter deal.

A RUNAWAY BEST SELLER

The first edition of *Uncle Tom's Cabin* went on sale on March 20, 1852, a few weeks before the last installment of the novel appeared in the *National Era*. The timing was meant to lure in readers of the serial who could not wait to read its end in the magazine. The ploy worked far better than Jewett or the Stowes had hoped. The success of the serial had suggested the book could sell well, but no one was prepared for its astounding popularity. On its first day on the market, *Uncle Tom's Cabin* sold thousands of copies. Jewett soon had to go back to press. As demand grew, he had paper mills and printing presses working around the clock to manufacture enough books to satisfy eager buyers. By the end of 1852, *Uncle Tom's Cabin* had sold an estimated 300,000 copies, a huge number in such a short amount of time. Even more impressive, each book was passed around from reader to reader. In many households, it was read out loud to the entire family for after-dinner entertainment. Scholars suggest that as many as 10 people read *Uncle Tom's Cabin* (or heard it read) for every copy sold. If that was the case, by the end of the year, 3 million Americans had been exposed to Stowe's novel, at a time when the total population of the United States was about 23 million.

Three months after *Uncle Tom's Cabin's* publication, Stowe received her first royalty check. By that time, her 10 percent

Uncle Tom's Cabin brought Harriet Beecher Stowe international fame. More than half a million copies were sold in the first five years in the United States and many stores had difficulty keeping the book in stock. Pictured is an 1852 store poster advertising the book.

share in the book had netted her $10,000 (about $300,000 in today's dollars). It was an astounding windfall for the struggling Stowes. In fact, the press noted that no author in the United States or Europe had ever made so much in royalty income so fast from a single work. Still, the amount left a slightly sour taste in Stowe's mouth. She wondered if Jewett had taken advantage of her by offering such a low royalty rate. Catharine Beecher certainly thought so. She said Stowe should sue Jewett and publicly expose him as a shyster. Stowe, though, decided not to take any action against Jewett. She probably, quite rightly, sensed that doing so would damage her public

"LITTLE EVA: UNCLE TOM'S GUARDIAN ANGEL"

On September 19, 1953, the *New York Daily Tribune* reported, "*Uncle Tom's Cabin* has become almost world-wide in its currency and fame. Songs founded on its more affecting incidents are beginning to be sung at nearly every house." One of the most popular was "Little Eva: Uncle Tom's Guardian Angel." John P. Jewett, Stowe's publisher, commissioned the song as a way of promoting the book. He paid the famous poet John Greenleaf Whittier $50 to write the lyrics, which focused on Eva, the most popular of Stowe's characters. Whittier told Stowe's readers not to cry over the death of Little Eva, because her ascent to heaven released her from all earthly "care and pain and weariness."

> *Dry the tears for holy Eva,*
> *With the blessed angels leave her,*
> *Of the form so sweet and fair*
> *Give to earth the tender care.*
>
> *For the golden locks of Eva*
> *Let the sunny southland give her*
> *Flowery pillow of repose*

image. Keeping that image unstained was now important not only to her personal honor but also to her pocketbook. Stowe did not want to do anything that would slow down the sales of her best seller.

In retrospect, Calvin's willingness to give away 10 percent of the novel's profits to finance the book's promotional budget

Orange bloom and budding rose,
Orange bloom and budding rose.

All is light and peace with Eva,
There the darkness cometh never,
Tears are wiped and fetters fall,
And the Lord is all in all.

Weep no more for happy Eva
Wrong and sin no more shall grieve her,
Care and pain and weariness
Lost in love so measureless,
Lost in love so measureless.

Gentle Eva loving Eva
Child confessor, true believer,
Listen'r at the Master's knee,
"Suffer such to come to me."

Oh for faith like thine, sweet Eva,
Lighting all the solemn river,
And the blessing of the poor
Wafting to the heavenly shore,
Wafting to the heavenly shore.

might have seemed foolish. But in fact, Jewett was a tireless promoter of the novel. Determined to milk every cent out of book, he published a cheap paperback edition for people too poor to afford the hardcover. He also brought out a version just for children, which proved very popular. For the Christmas season, Jewett prepared an elaborate gift edition with more than 100 original engravings.

THE UNCLE TOM CRAZE

Each of Jewett's editions added money to Stowe's coffers. But she did not see a dime from editions published in Europe, because at the time there were no international copyright laws. She also did not receive any money from a new industry she helped to create—the manufacture and sale of memorabilia and merchandise relating to *Uncle Tom's Cabin*. Americans who embraced her novel could not seem to get enough of Uncle Tom, Little Eva, and her other characters. Their images appeared on little statues, wallpaper, dishware, and toys. (One of the many "Uncle Tom" games had players compete to reunite slave families.) The sheet music of songs based on scenes from the novel were also extremely popular.

At least in the North, Americans' fascination with *Uncle Tom's Cabin* seemed to cross all boundaries. A reviewer in *Literary World* described the national mania focused on the novel: "No age or sex is spared, men and women and children all confess its power. No condition is exempt; lords and ladies, flunkies and kitchen-maids are equally infected with the rage. The prevailing affection is universal, and all have Uncle Tom, whether at rest or in motion, at leisure or at work, on the rail or in the idle repose of the parlor, or in the busy bustle of the kitchen."

The book was a popular sensation, but even the literary giants of the day were not immune to its charms. In his journal, the famed poet Henry Wadsworth Longfellow recorded that he had begun Stowe's "pathetic and droll book on slavery."

Two weeks later, he was no longer so dismissive of the novel. He wrote that "every evening we read our selves into despair in that tragic book, 'Uncle Tom's Cabin.' It is too melancoly, and makes one's blood boil too hotly."

THE ABOLITIONISTS WEIGH IN

Despite the wildly enthusiastic response to *Uncle Tom's Cabin*, Stowe had her share of detractors. Among them were some Northern clergymen, who Stowe had taken to task for not campaigning for the abolitionist cause as ferociously as her famous brother Henry had. She cited one minister by name, Joel Parker, who then initiated a libel suit against her. In correspondence between Stowe and Parker, it was clear that Parker was not only angry that, by his estimation, she had besmirched his good name, he was also offended, as were a number of prominent ministers, that a woman would dare to criticize his morality in a public forum.

Perhaps surprisingly, given the attention *Uncle Tom's Cabin* drew to the antislavery cause, most abolitionists showed little enthusiasm for the book. (An exception was the well-known abolitionist William Lloyd Garrison, who wrote a largely positive review of Stowe's novel in his newspaper *The Liberator*.) They regarded Stowe as an outsider, because she had never worked closely with an antislavery organization. There was also probably some resentment among male abolitionists that a woman writer, coming virtually out of nowhere, could so stir up the country about a cause they had devoted their lives to promoting.

Some abolitionists were truly offended by the end of *Uncle Tom's Cabin*, in which George Harris, a slave who has escaped to Canada, decides to take his family and move to the African country of Liberia. Liberia had been founded by the American Colonization Society in 1822 as a place where freed African-American slaves could be sent. The idea of sending all ex-slaves to Africa—a policy called colonization—was disgusting in the eyes of many prominent abolitionists. It catered to the worst prejudices of white Americans who considered blacks as inherently inferior. The proponents of colonization thought that blacks and whites could and should not live together peaceably, hence their insistence that all ex-slaves be resettled outside of the borders of the United States. By the 1850s, most abolitionists had rejected the colonization policy as racist. They believed that ex-slaves should not be banished from the country for the sins of their slave owners. Instead, they held that freed slaves should be assimilated into the larger American society.

To these abolitionists, Harris's decision to move to Africa seemed like an endorsement of the colonization policy. But, most likely, Stowe did not mean it as such. (After all, as presented in the book, it is Harris's personal decision, not one the narrator prescribes for all freed slaves.) Stowe was not well versed in the beliefs of the various factions within the abolitionist movement, so she probably was unaware of the vehement opposition to colonization. She most likely was merely echoing the views of her father, Lyman Beecher, who supported both abolition and colonization, but who was not a leader in the larger antislavery movement. In any case, Stowe soon regretted her seeming endorsement of colonization. In 1853, just a year after the novel's publication, she said that if she had it to do over again, she would not mention colonization in the book at all.

Uncle Tom's Cabin also set off a spirited debate among African-American abolitionists. The most famous, Frederick Douglass, publicly praised Stowe's work, although he did offer some gentle criticism of the book. Irked by its suggested support of colonization, he took Stowe to task on the issue in a public letter: "The truth is, dear madame, we are here, and here we are likely to remain." A much harsher critic was Martin R. Delany. In *Frederick Douglass's Paper*, he criticized Stowe for thinking she somehow could speak for African Americans. He claimed, "she knows nothing about us, the free colored people of the United States." Responding to Delany, Douglass took a generous stance, citing "Mrs. Stowe's power to do us good" and reminding Delany of the worth of "recogniz[ing] friends wherever we find them."

STOWE'S SOUTHERN CRITICS

Predictably, Stowe's harshest critics were from the South. The kindest offered some praise for the novel as entertainment, while emphasizing that Stowe presented a completely inaccurate view of Southern life and of the institution of slavery. But few responses were so measured. Most Southerners who read *Uncle Tom's Cabin* were enraged that a Northern woman had the audacity to write a book lambasting their way of life and their culture.

One means of discrediting Stowe was to attack her gentility. By writing about vulgar and disgusting subjects, they said she had revealed herself to be vulgar and disgusting. A reviewer in the *New Orleans Crescent* described Stowe as "part quack and part cut-throat. There never before was anything so detestable or so monstrous among women as this." William G. Brownlow, a minister from Knoxville, Tennessee, offered attacks on Stowe so extreme that they soon became notorious. In the *Whig and Independent Journal*, he recounted his revulsion on just seeing a photograph of Stowe: "[She is] as ugly as Original sin—an abomination in the eyes of civilized people. . . . [She is a] tall, coarse, vulgar-looking woman—stoop-shouldered with a long yellow neck, and a long peaked nose—through which she speaks."

Although such personal attacks were common, the most popular complaint from Southerners was that Stowe got her facts wrong. Slavery, they said, was not an evil institution that subjugated blacks. It was instead part of a benevolent society that recognized the truth that African Americans were inferior and incapable of taking care of themselves without the help of kindly whites. Furthermore, Southern reviews held that Stowe's presentation of the whippings and beatings of slaves was highly exaggerated. According to these reviews, slave owners rarely resorted to such extreme measures and, when they did, it was clearly because disobedient slaves deserved to be punished.

Many Southern critics focused on Stowe's characters, especially Uncle Tom and George Harris. Stowe's Uncle Tom was exceptionally pious—so much so that Stowe presented his death as that of a Christian martyr. Southern reviewers often argued that Tom was unrealistic, because blacks were incapable of understanding and embracing Christianity to the extent that Tom did. Similarly, they dismissed her representation of George Harris. Blacks were simple people, they said, making Harris's intelligence an obvious and egregious flaw in Stowe's fictional world.

ANTI-TOM NOVELS

For some Southern writers, negative reviews were not enough to combat Stowe's message. They resorted to writing entire novels to challenge *Uncle Tom's Cabin*. These books, known as anti-Tom novels, included such works as Mary H. Eastman's *Aunt Phillis's Cabin* (1852) and Robert Criswell's *Uncle Tom's Cabin Contrasted with Buckingham Hall, the Planter's Home* (1852).

Although the anti-Tom novels differed in plot and tone, they generally had some features in common. Slave owners were always kind and upright, while their wives were always gentle and beautiful. The books usually presented only two types of slaves. One type were slaves unfailingly loyal to their masters. These slave characters were sometimes given a final deathbed scene, during which they emotionally thanked their owners for treating them so wonderfully. The other type were slaves who rebelled against their masters. They were presented as surly and stupid, too foolish to see how well they lived under slavery. Abolitionists occasionally made cameos in the anti-Tom novels. They were sometimes presented as deluded do-gooders, but more often as evil meddlers. Some of these abolitionist characters were involved in the antislavery

Mary Henderson Eastman developed close relationships with the Dakota Sioux and learned their language. She published several books that expressed anger at white treatment of American Indians. Yet, Eastman was outraged by *Uncle Tom's Cabin* and, in response, wrote a positive portrait of slave life in *Aunt Phillis's Cabin; or, Southern Life As It Is*, which became one of the most popular of the anti-Tom novels. Eastman later changed her mind about slavery and became a Unionist.

movement only because they saw it as an avenue for seducing slave women.

Another gimmick of the anti-Tom novels was to take specific scenes in Stowe's book and recast them from a Southern slave owner's perspective. Especially popular were reimaginings of Eva teaching Tom to read the Bible. In Stowe's work, Tom's education was taken seriously and presented as proof of his deep religious piety. In the anti-Tom novels, the scene was played for laughs, lampooning the very idea that blacks could ever be taught to read, to think, or to understand the Christian faith.

A KEY TO UNCLE TOM'S CABIN

The Southern reaction to *Uncle Tom's Cabin* was sometimes almost humorously shrill. Nevertheless, it got under Stowe's skin enough that she felt compelled to respond. She enlisted her friends and family into helping her assemble documentary evidence that would convince everyone of the accuracy of her work and, by extension, of the dishonesty of the Southerners who condemned it. She originally intended to collect the material in a 100-page appendix to *Uncle Tom's Cabin*. Instead, she wrote a 259-page book titled *A Key to Uncle Tom's Cabin*, which was published by John P. Jewett in 1853.

Stowe presented the documents in *Key* as the source material she had used when writing *Uncle Tom's Cabin*. But in truth, most of it she read only after her novel was published. In fact, Stowe was taken aback by her research on *Key*, from which she learned new details about the horrors of slavery. In a letter to her friend Lord Denman, she wrote, "[I]t is worse than I supposed or dreamed."

If Stowe really believed that *Key* would end the personal attacks from Southern reviewers, she was certainly naïve. If anything, it only inflamed the viciousness directed toward her. Many reviewers of *Key* condemned Stowe not for presenting falsehoods about slavery, but for daring to discuss the terrible truths of the institution, particularly the all-too-common forced sexual relationships between male masters and female slaves. One critic, George Frederick Holmes, declared that Stowe's crime of writing about these unsavory matters was just as immoral as the abuses themselves: "Grant that every accusation brought by Mrs. Stowe is perfectly true, that every vice alleged occurs as she has represented, the pollution of such literature to the heart and mind of women is not less." Another reviewer, William Gilmore Simms, writing in the *Southern Quarterly Review*, declared, "Mrs. Stowe betrays a malignity so remarkable that the petticoats lifts of itself, and we see the hoof of the beast under the table." He suggested what many Southerners believed—that *Uncle Tom's Cabin* and Stowe's public defense of it were proof that she was no better than the devil himself.

6

The War Years

With the enormous success of *Uncle Tom's Cabin*, Harriet Beecher Stowe found herself in a difficult position. She was now the leading voice for the abolition of slavery in the United States, while at the same time she had never been part of any of the organizations that had driven the antislavery movement. To the uninitiated, like Stowe, the politics of the movement were complex and hard to grasp, as each organization competed with the others for members and support. Stowe wisely shied away from allying herself to any one group, although given her notoriety, she would certainly have been welcomed by any organization looking to influence the public debate.

Stowe's gender also restricted what she could do for the abolitionist cause. It was considered inappropriate for a woman to speak publicly about politics, and Stowe was very concerned about her image. She saw that her career and livelihood depended on it. Her readers wanted to think of Stowe as a "good" woman, which then meant that she had to appear morally upright, modest, and self-effacing.

Stowe expertly presented such a persona in a letter to children's book author Eliza Cabot Follon. Responding to Follon's request that she provide a little personal information about herself, Stowe wrote, "I am a little bit of a woman—somewhat more than 40—about as thin & dry as a pinch of snuff never very much to look at in my best days—& looking like a used-up article now." She also went out of her way to explain that she had not sought out the fame and fortune she enjoyed, because professional ambition would have appeared unseemly in a woman. She claimed that she began writing just so she could afford a few household amenities, such as a featherbed, when in fact her earnings were important to the household income. Despite her talent for self-promotion, she held that she was loath to see images of herself published: "[I]f you ever get to see a wood cut of me, with an inordinately long nose, on the cover of all the Anti Slavery almanacs, I wish you take notice that I have been forced into it, contrary to my natural modesty by the imperative solicitations of my dear 5000 friends & the public generally."

BRITISH WOMEN JOIN THE CAUSE

In Great Britain, Stowe's self-description was copied down and passed around among her many fans. Somewhat surprisingly, *Uncle Tom's Cabin* had even more readers in Great Britain than in the United States. By 1853, sales there had reached about 1.5 million. Stage productions of the book were wildly popular, and thousands of boys and girls learned the story of Uncle Tom through a special Sunday school edition of the novel.

The popularity of Stowe's book prompted an unprecedented political action among the women of Great Britain. Three

After reading *Uncle Tom's Cabin*, thousands of people supported the abolitionists' cause in America and abroad. In 1853, Stowe went on a speaking tour to promote the book in Europe, where she was embraced and presented with an anti-slavery petition that had the signatures of more than half a million women of all classes. This depiction shows Stowe at a public reading in London.

nobles—the Duchess of Sutherland, the Earl of Shaftesbury, and the Earl of Carlisle—drew up a petition titled "An Affectionate and Christian Address of Many Thousands of Women of Great Britain and Ireland to Their Sisters the Women of the United States of America." The petition was a plea by the women of Great Britain to the women of the United States, asking them to rise up and oppose slavery in their land. It contended, as *Uncle Tom's Cabin* had done, that the institution of slavery was immoral because it broke up slave families, devalued marriages between slaves, and prohibited slaves from obtaining the education they needed to become devout Christians. Circulated from house to house, the petition was signed by more than half a million women.

In the spring of 1853, Stowe was invited by two women's antislavery groups to receive the petition in person. Accompanied by Calvin and her brother Charles, she boarded a ship bound for England. As the ship approached shore, she saw an enormous crowd assembled on the dock. It was made up of fans who had all come out hoping to get a glimpse of the famous author of *Uncle Tom's Cabin*. Wherever Stowe went during her trip, she was similarly greeted by well-wishers. In his journal, Charles Beecher recorded, "At every place where the cars stop, crowds are waiting. She cannot go out to ride nor show her face without crowds & hurrahs."

CELEBRATING STOWE

While in Great Britain, Stowe was feted at a series of celebrations held in her honor. At one dinner party, hosted by the mayor of London, she met the beloved English novelist Charles Dickens, who was known for his sympathetic portraits of the city's poor. The mayor hailed both Stowe and Dickens for writing fiction that drew attention to the suffering of oppressed peoples in their native countries.

But Stowe's most extraordinary invitation was offered by the Duchess of Sutherland. At the end of her tour of Great Britain,

Stowe arrived at the duchess's mansion to receive the antislavery petition her novel had inspired. The petition's signatures filled 26 bound volumes. Stowe also received a gold bracelet in the shape of a slave's wrist shackle. It was inscribed with the date that slavery was abolished in the British Empire. A space on the bracelet was left blank so that Stowe could have it engraved with the date the United States followed suit. During the ceremony, Stowe offered the solemn prediction that she was unlikely to see that day: "The memorial you placed on my wrist will ever be dear to me—mournfully dear—I may not live to have engraved there the glorious date of emancipation in America but my *children will* if I do not—& I trust *that date* shall yet be added to this chain."

After a visit to France and Germany, Stowe headed home in early September. She returned with more than her bracelet and petition. In Great Britain, she had also received a collection taken up by her British female fans. They were upset that Stowe had received no money for the copies of her book sold in Great Britain. To right this wrong, each reader was asked to contribute a penny to Stowe. Because of the "Penny Offering," Stowe left Great Britain $20,000 richer.

BLEEDING KANSAS

During her travels, Stowe promised fans that she would mobilize the women of America just as the Duchess of Sutherland had the women of Great Britain. The Penny Offering only added to her determination to rally American women to the antislavery cause. Although the money was given to Stowe with no instructions on how to spend it, she knew people would expect her to use at least part of it to fund the antislavery movement.

Stowe cast about, trying to find some way of furthering the cause. She envisioned a national organization of women against slavery, headed by her sister Catharine, but it never got off the ground. She made plans for establishing schools for African-American teachers in the North; however, when factions in the movement questioned how her idea would help abolish slavery, she lost interest. In the end, while Stowe offered money to individual ex-slaves in need, she failed to find a way to use her clout to mobilize her fan base. In essence, her natural talents and temperament suited her to a career as a writer, not a career as an activist.

Probably recognizing this in herself, Stowe returned to writing fiction about the issue of slavery. While she was beginning work on her next novel, abolitionists were fuming over a new abomination—the passage of the Kansas-Nebraska Act of 1854. The new law allowed the people of Kansas and Nebraska to determine for themselves whether or not to make slavery legal in their state. To tip the balance in Kansas, abolitionists organized the Emigrant Aid Society, which sent Northerners to live in the new state in order to vote against slavery there. At Henry Ward Beecher's church in Brooklyn, parishioners sent boxes of rifles (nicknamed Beecher's Bibles) to help Kansas's antislavery forces protect themselves from proslavery settlers who were flooding across the Missouri-Kansas border.

By late 1855, the two groups were warring against each other. An attack on the antislavery town of Lawrence was followed by a massacre of five proslavery settlers by a band led by abolitionist John Brown. The violence earned the state a new nickname—Bleeding Kansas.

DRED AND *THE MINISTER'S WOOING*

Stowe wrote the Duchess of Argyle, whom she had met in England, about how the events in Kansas influenced her new novel *Dred: A Tale of the Great Dismal Swamp* (1856): "The book is written under the impulse of our stormy times, how . . . the sack of Lawrence burn within us I hope to make a voice to say." *Dred* tells the story of the relationship between whites and slaves on a North Carolina plantation. The title character is an escaped slave who has fled into nearby swamplands. Perhaps in response to criticism of Uncle Tom's passivity, Dred is a fiery character who advocates violent revenge on slave owners.

Stowe wrote *Dred* in just over three months, sometimes firing off as many as 25 pages a day. Her haste shows. The story meanders, and her characters are not fully developed. Even Calvin recognized the novel's deficiencies and suggested that she slow down her writing pace. As he wrote Stowe, "*Dred . . .* has too many pimples on its face."

Although it was not a sensation like *Uncle Tom's Cabin*, *Dred* sold fairly well. To make sure she earned her due, Stowe had negotiated a contract with a new publisher, giving her 50 percent of the profits. She also took another trip to Europe, specifically to obtain the international copyright for *Dred* in her name. In time, Stowe earned about $20,000 from her second novel.

After returning home, Stowe grew worried about her teenage son Fred, who had developed a drinking problem. But her eldest son, Henry, soon caused her even greater anguish. A student at Dartmouth College, Henry was swimming in the Connecticut River with some classmates when a strong current carried him away. Stowe was distraught by Henry's death. In a letter, her sister-in-law Isabella wrote that Stowe told her, "Henry was the only one of our children that we had begun not to feel anxious for & to hope to rely on him ourselves." The tragedy influenced her next novel, *The Minister's Wooing* (1859). The book was a period piece set in New England during the 1790s. A gentle satire on the Calvinist religion Stowe grew up with, it pointedly criticized ministers who instructed the grieving on how to act, rather than allowing them to trust their own feelings.

WORKING WITH THE *ATLANTIC MONTHLY*

The Minister's Wooing was serialized in a new magazine called the *Atlantic Monthly*. It was founded by a group of New England intellectuals who wanted to define American literary culture. Associating herself with the magazine benefited Stowe (at least initially) because its writers were promoted as the leading liter-

The *Atlantic Monthly* magazine was founded in 1857 in Boston by a group of writers that included Ralph Waldo Emerson, Henry Wadsworth Longfellow, Oliver Wendell Holmes Sr., and James Russell Lowell. When Stowe became famous, she was invited to publish her writings in the magazine, and she became the magazine's most celebrated woman writer.

ary figures of the day. In turn, the *Atlantic* editors were eager to attach Stowe's name to the magazine because of her popularity with the reading public.

Stowe also had an unusual instinct for sensing what her audience wanted to read. Her next novel for the *Atlantic*, for instance, was one of the first examples of a new American literary genre—the international novel. Newly wealthy Americans were increasingly interested in European travel. Her novel *Agnes of Sorrento* (1862), set in exotic Italy, tapped into this vogue.

Stowe used her earnings from her writing to construct a large house in Hartford, Connecticut, which she called Oakholm. Without regard to its cost in time and money, she threw herself into managing teams of laborers to build the house precisely to her specifications. At the same time, to pay for her project, she took on more writing work than she could handle. While she was churning out chapter after chapter of *Agnes*, she was also writing a coming-of-age novel titled *The Pearl of Orr's Island* (1862) for the *Independent*, a large New York newspaper. Exhausted by her harried writing schedule, Stowe soon told the *Independent* that she could not keep up with her commitments. At her request, *Pearl* was put on hold in the middle of its serialization, not to be resumed until *Agnes* was complete.

WAR BREAKS OUT

While Stowe was agonizing over deadlines, the United States was facing a crisis. In November 1860, Abraham Lincoln was elected president of the United States. His Republican Party vowed to stop the expansion of slavery, a position that infuriated Southern leaders. Many began talking about Southern states seceding (declaring independence from) the Union. The first state to secede was South Carolina; six others—Mississippi, Florida, Alabama, Georgia, Louisiana, and Texas—soon followed its example. In February 1861, these seven Southern states, calling themselves the Confederate States of America, established their own government. (In the months that followed, four more states—North Carolina, Virginia, Arkansas, and Tennessee—joined the Confederacy.)

MORAL AUTHORITY AND STOWE'S WOMEN READERS

Just before she began work on *Uncle Tom's Cabin*, Harriet Beecher Stowe wrote to her sister Catharine about a visit she had with one of her closest friends, Thomas Upham, a professor at Bowdoin College: "He and I had over the tea table the other night that sort of an argument which consists of both sides saying over & over just what they said before." The topic was the Fugitive Slave Act, which prohibited Northerners from helping runaway slaves in any way. Stowe was determined to speak out against the law, while Upham wanted to "avoid all agitation." Finally, Stowe asked him point blank whether he would obey the law. While Upham "hemmed & hawed," his young daughter Mary interrupted him, declaring, to Stowe's delight, "I wouldn't, I know."

A version of the anecdote appears in Chapter 9 of *Uncle Tom's Cabin*, in which John Bird, an Ohio senator, and his wife, Mary, discuss the Fugitive Slave Act. Like Upham, the senator hems and haws over his feelings about the controversial law. His wife, however, like Mary Upham, does not have to think twice about the matter: She knows instinctively that the law is morally wrong and, therefore, she has no obligation to obey it. As she tells her husband, "Now, John, I don't know anything about politics, but I can read my Bible; and there I see that I must feed the hungry, clothe the naked, and comfort the desolate; and that Bible I mean to follow."

The scene highlights one of most important themes of Stowe's work—that women can exert a powerful influence on the world by promoting moral principles within the

(continues)

(continued)

home. *Uncle Tom's Cabin* emboldened women by encouraging them to see themselves as their family's moral authority. Some readers were inspired to exercise that authority by actively joining the antislavery movement. But many more chose a less public role, using their moral compass to instruct their children in what was right and what was wrong. In this quiet way, *Uncle Tom's Cabin* may have had its greatest impact on the politics of the era. Remembering how many mothers read the book and communicated its message to their sons, Pulitzer Prize-winning historian James Ford Rhodes made this case in his *History of the United States* (1892): "The great influence of Mrs. Stowe's book . . . was shown in bringing home to the hearts of the people the conviction that slavery is an injustice; and, indeed, the impression it made upon bearded men was not so powerful as its appeal to women and boys. The mother's opinion was a potent educator in politics between 1852 and 1860, and boys in their teens in the one year were voters in the other."

After Lincoln's inauguration, tensions between the Union and the Confederacy came to a head. On April 12, 1861, Confederate troops fired on U.S. soldiers stationed at Fort Sumter in South Carolina. The shots were the first fired in what would become the four-year national nightmare now called the American Civil War.

Some predicted the war would soon be over, but Stowe feared that the South would not give up the fight easily. Writing in the *Independent*, she envisioned "a long, grave period of severe self-denial . . . which will task the resources, physical, mental and moral, of our Northern States." Adding to her anxiety over the future of the nation were more personal concerns about her troubled son Fred. A medical student, Fred quit school to enlist in the Union (Northern) army. Like any soldier's mother, Stowe worried that Fred would be sent into combat. She also fretted over his spending time in rough military camps, where he might be lured back into heavy drinking.

Although she had decided to delay writing the conclusion of *Pearl* before the war began, Stowe justified her decision to the *Independent* readership by citing her wartime sorrows: "Who could write stories, that had a son to send to battle, with Washington beleaguered, and the whole country shaken as with an earthquake?" Even so, Stowe managed to keep writing *Agnes*, as well as opinion pieces about the war for the *Independent*. By mid-1862, she had joined a chorus of voices demanding that President Abraham Lincoln free the slaves. She wrote, "The time has come when the nation has a RIGHT to demand, and the President of the United States a right to decree, their freedom; and there should go up petitions from all the land that he should do it."

MEETING LINCOLN

Lincoln responded to these critics by saying, "My paramount object in this struggle is to save the Union." The comment so angered Stowe that she issued a blistering reply in the *Independent*: "My paramount object in this struggle is to set at liberty them that are bruised, and not either to save or destroy the Union. What I do in favor of the Union, I do because it helps to free the oppressed; what I forbear, I forbear because it would hurt the cause of the slave, and more when I believe it would help the cause of the slave."

In September 1862, Lincoln issued a preliminary version of the Emancipation Proclamation. This document was what abolitionists like Stowe had long fought for. It declared that Washington would free the slaves of any Confederate state that

During the Civil War, Stowe grew impatient with President Lincoln, who was most concerned with preserving the Union. She began to call for more radical actions to end slavery. In 1862, Stowe went to see Lincoln to pressure him to free the slaves. It has been claimed (and also refuted) that Lincoln said, upon meeting Stowe, "So you're the little lady that started this great war."

did not rejoin the Union by January 1, 1863. When she had received the antislavery petition in Great Britain in 1853, Stowe said she doubted she would live to see the abolition of slavery in America. Now she made plans to engrave Lincoln's deadline on the gold shackle bracelet she was given during that trip.

Stowe also began preparing for a trip to Washington. Fred's regiment was stationed there, and she was eager to see how he was holding up. During her trip, she not only visited Fred, but also toured the barracks of fugitive slaves who had joined the Union army. Stowe was moved by the sight of hundreds of African-American soldiers joined in singing the spiritual "Go Down, Moses." She noted they delivered the last line of the chorus—"Let My People Go"—with great emotion.

Stowe had another reason for going to Washington. She wanted to talk with influential people to make sure that Lincoln was serious about freeing the slaves before writing about the matter in the *Independent*. In a letter to her *Atlantic* editor, James Fields, Stowe wrote, "It seems to be the opinion that the president will stand up to his Proclamation." A few days later, she got a chance to assess Lincoln's intentions directly: She received an invitation to meet with the president and his wife. On December 2, she and her daughter Hatty were welcomed to the White House. There is no record of what was said, but a letter from Hatty to her twin suggests that it was a peculiar meeting: "It was a very droll time that we had at the White house I assure you. . . . I will only say now that it was all very funny—and we were ready to explode with laughter all the while." Stowe herself wrote Calvin that they had had a "real funny interview," promising to tell him all about it when she returned home.

THE HEAD OF THE HOUSEHOLD

In 1863, 61-year-old Calvin Stowe retired from teaching. The decision brought great change to the Stowe household. From then on, Harriet would be the family's sole breadwinner. She welcomed the challenge, confident that she could make up for Calvin's lost salary. As she wrote her eldest daughters Hatty and Eliza, "Now it is very easy for me to write. Writing is my element as much as sailing is to a duck." But Stowe also recognized that the more writing she did, the less time she had for housekeeping. The twins, who up until then had lived a pampered life, were going have to take up the slack. "You cannot make money," Stowe explained, "but you can set my mind free to make it for you."

Stowe was frustrated by Hatty's and Eliza's frivolous natures, but her other children were causing her more serious anguish. Georgiana was excessively moody, excitable one moment and depressed the next. Her behavior was mostly due to a dependence on morphine, prescribed to her by doctors. She would never fully overcome her addiction.

Stowe's youngest child, Charley, was spoiled and bratty. Hoping to instill in him some discipline and self-control, she enrolled him in a military boarding school. Charley ran away from the school, headed for the port city of Bridgeport, Connecticut, and signed up to work on a ship. When his parents found out, they chased him down in Bridgeport and brought him home. For a few weeks, they tried to convince him to go to business school, but Charley insisted on a life at sea. The Stowes finally gave up, and Charley set sail for Italy with his parents' blessing.

Fred, however, remained their greatest worry, especially after he was wounded at Gettysburg in July 1863. During the brutal battle, a piece of shell entered his ear. Appealing directly to the secretary of war, Edwin M. Stanton, Stowe had Fred transferred to a hospital in New York, where she helped nurse him back to health. But Fred never fully recovered from his war injury. He would experience excruciating headaches for the rest of his life.

THE END OF THE WAR

Fred's ordeal and the horrific news from the battlefield were overwhelming to Stowe. As she wrote to Fields, "I feel I need to write in these days to keep from thinking of things that make me dizzy & blind & fill my eyes with tears. . . . I feel the need of a little gentle household merriment & talk of common things." She proposed a series of pieces for the *Atlantic* called the "House and Home Papers."

Throughout 1864, while the war raged, Stowe wrote quaint columns about how best to choose a carpet or arrange furniture in the parlor, once again displaying her uncanny instinct for what her audience wanted. The "House and Home Papers," which readers embraced as a welcome relief from war news, were a great success. Bolstered by the series' popularity, Stowe continued to concentrate on writing lighter fare, including children's books and sketches about her travels in Italy.

On April 9, 1865, after four years of bloody warfare, the Confederate Army finally surrendered in Appomattox, Virginia. At last, the Civil War was over. The Union was preserved, and the blight of slavery had come to an end. Stowe reacted to the news by revisiting *Uncle Tom's Cabin*, the book that had done so much to stoke the antislavery fervor that anticipated the great war. She wrote the Duchess of Argyle about the emotions she felt as she reread her novel after the conflict's conclusion: "[W]hen I read that book scarred & seared & burned into with the memories of an anguish & horror that can never be forgotten & think it is all over now!—all past!—& that now the questions debated are simply of more or less time before granting legal suffrage to these who so lately were held only as articles of dead merchandise—When this comes over me—I think no private or individual sorrow, can ever make me wholly without comfort."

Later Work and Final Days

With the tumultuous war years behind them, the Stowes returned their attention to problems closer to home. Their first concern was finding a meaningful occupation for their son Fred. Stowe invested in a cotton plantation in Florida, which Fred was to operate with two partners. The plan for Fred's rehabilitation did not succeed. In July 1867, he showed up at the Stowes' Hartford home in worse shape than ever. As a final attempt to get his alcoholism under control, Fred agreed to enter a mental institution.

For Stowe, there was one silver lining in this latest desperate attempt to help her son. She fell in love with the beautiful landscapes and pleasant climate of Florida and resolved to spend her winters there. At the time, Northerners had just begun to buy vacation homes in the state. Fearful that if she

In 1867, the Stowe family bought a cottage in the town of Mandarin, Florida. For the next 17 years Harriet escaped the harsh winters of New England, finding refuge in her modest Mandarin home. She came to love the land and the people of Florida. Stowe produced a series of sketches based on the experiences in the state called *Palmetto Leaves* (1873).

did not act fast real estate prices would rise too high, Stowe impulsively set down $5,000 for a cottage and an orange grove in the town of Mandarin.

In the winter, Florida seemed like a paradise to Stowe. Although she loved New England, given her small frame, she had always found the coldest months extremely hard for her body to take. Spending winters in Florida, however, was no easy undertaking. Every year, the family had to scurry around for weeks to close down the Hartford house for the winter, ship books and furniture to Mandarin, and, once they had arrived by train, unpack and set up house in their Florida home.

OLDTOWN FOLKS

Following the war, Stowe's first big project was a new novel she titled *Oldtown Folks* (1869). It was a chronicle of the lives of the people of Natick, Massachusetts—Calvin's hometown. Much of it was based on the stories of his youth.

Oldtown Folks was one of the few novels Stowe wrote that was not serialized before publication. She spent a good deal of time on the book, most likely in response to a shift in the American literary scene. Increasingly, a small group of male editors and critics (such as those associated with the *Atlantic*) were viewed as the ultimate judges of quality in American fiction. In the past, Stowe had wanted only to please her readers. Now she was also seeking the approval of these self-appointed literary tastemakers.

The strategy backfired. *Oldtown Folks* was one of her weakest novels, long and unfocused, lacking the energy of her best work. Joan D. Hedrick, author of *Harriet Beecher Stowe: A Life* (1994), suggests that the writing suffered because, without serializing the work, Stowe did not get the ongoing feedback from readers that often helped shape her narratives. According to Hedrick, "While there is some very good writing and good dialect in *Oldtown Folks*, Stowe's distance from her audience dulled her ear and her awareness of how far she could stretch the reader's tolerance."

Stowe's hope to win over the literary establishment also failed. Most reviews were bad, and many were laced with a blatant antiwoman bias. As prominent male writers were taking over the American literary scene, they grew dismissive of the works of female writers, even one as prominent and beloved as Stowe. They argued that the concerns of women, often focusing on the family and the community, were trivial compared to the more worldly concerns of men. But despite the bad reviews, *Oldtown Folks* sold a respectable 25,000 copies, proving that Stowe's loyal readers were less interested than Stowe herself about what the critics had to say.

THE WOMEN'S RIGHTS MOVEMENT

While dealing with the misogyny of the new literary leadership, Stowe was also exposed to the ideas of the burgeoning women's rights movement. Two of the movement's leaders, Elizabeth Cady Stanton and Susan B. Anthony, made a point of contacting Stowe and her half sister Isabella Beecher Hooker, who was already sympathetic to their cause. Stanton and Anthony wanted Stowe and Hooker to sign on as editor and associate editor of their magazine, *The Revolution*.

They felt that getting Stowe involved with their movement would help broaden its appeal to her many female fans. As Anthony wrote a colleague, "her *name is good.*" But Anthony also recognized that the fight for women's rights might provide Stowe with an even better subject than abolitionism had: "*Mrs. Stowe—even—*has never *yet given to the world her very best*—for she nor any other woman can, until she *writes direct* out of *her own souls experience.*"

Stowe and Hooker met with the two women's rights activists in August 1869. In the end, however, they felt that *The Revolution* was a little too radical for them. They declined the

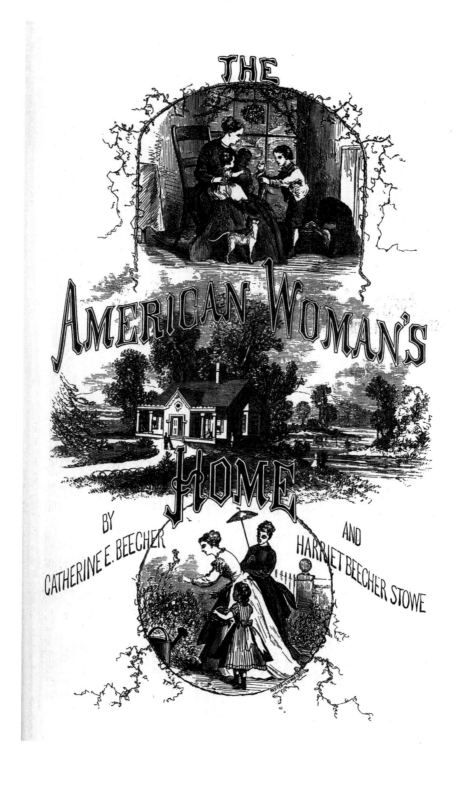

editorial posts, although they did agree to contribute an occasional piece to the magazine.

DEFENDING LADY BYRON

Stowe's brush with the women's rights movement, however, did help inspire her next work. A common complaint of women's rights activists was that married women had virtually no legal rights, which made it difficult for a woman to leave a marriage no matter how badly she was treated by her husband. In contemplating this, Stowe recalled the situation of her friend Lady Byron, whom she had met during her second trip to England. Lady Byron had been legally separated from her husband, the famous poet Lord Byron. She was widely ridiculed in the press for her rejection of Lord Byron, but refused to comment on it publicly. In confidence, she told Stowe a shocking story: Lord Byron had been conducting an incestuous affair with his half sister Augusta Leigh, and as a result Lady Byron could no longer live with him.

Stowe advised Lady Byron not to speak out, convinced that her reputation would never recover if she told others what had happened. Lady Byron agreed and died without ever revealing the secrets of her married life. But now, many years later, Stowe came to wonder about the worth of staying silent. She decided to take up Lady Byron's cause in print, thus giving voice to all married women scared of revealing similar indignities. She

(Opposite page) Throughout their lives Catharine Beecher and Harriet Beecher Stowe continued to support women's rights. Catharine fought for increased recognition of the work women did in managing their households and raising their families, which she felt was just as important as the work men did outside the home. In 1869, the sisters worked together on *The American Woman's Home*, the sequel to Catharine's best-selling *Treatise on Domestic Economy*.

wrote to Fields at the *Atlantic*, explaining why she wanted to write an article in defense of Lady Byron: "I tremble at what I am doing & saying but I feel that justice demands it of me & I *must* not fail."

Stowe predicted that her article "The True Story of Lady Byron's Life" would be a sensation. But she grossly underestimated the response. Characteristic of the press reviews was one in the *Independent*, which called her story "disgusting and obscene." Reviewers attacked Stowe for daring to mention incest, certainly not a subject a respectable woman should even know about. They also dragged the late Lady Byron once again through the mud, declaring that she had to have been insane to make such an accusation against her husband.

Stowe was stunned by the hostile reception of her article, but instead of trying to minimize this blow to her public image, she chose to dig herself into an even deeper hole. As she had with *A Key to Uncle Tom's Cabin*, she enlisted her family to help her compile a justification of her controversial work. The result was *Lady Byron Vindicated* (1870), a book-length defense of Lady Byron and, by extension, of Stowe. The mish-mash of documentation, however, did not in fact vindicate Stowe's friend. All it did was further tarnish the author's reputation. After the Lady Byron debacle, Stowe forever retreated from writing about sexual issues.

THE BEECHER-TILTON SCANDAL

In 1870, Henry Ward Beecher began publishing a newspaper called the *Christian Union*. He invited both Calvin and Harriet to write regular columns. The *Union* also serialized Harriet Beecher Stowe's next three novels—*My Wife and I* (1871), *Pink and White Tyranny* (1871), and *We and Our Neighbors* (1875). These novels were relatively light satires of society life. *My Wife and I*, however, was notable for a character who was clearly a satirical version of Victoria Woodhull. As flamboyant as she was infamous, Woodhull was an advocate of free love—that is, sexual relations between men and women outside the bounds of marriage.

Stowe's caricature had a hand in provoking Woodhull to make a stunning public declaration. In 1872, she accused Henry Ward Beecher of committing adultery with one of his parishioners, Elizabeth Tilton. The accusation was the beginning of the greatest sex scandal in nineteenth-century America. For years, newspapers and tabloids carried salacious speculations about what had happened between Henry and Elizabeth. The Beechers were of course infuriated by what they saw as an attack on the family honor. Unsurprisingly, Stowe took up Henry's case, arguing that her little brother was far too innocent to be involved in anything so tawdry. As she wrote to a cousin, "he is more angel than brother—he is too good for me—I sit and think all over his sorrow, all the injustice that was at one time done him—& all his gentle childlike tendencies of heart." The adultery charge was examined in a church investigation and a civil lawsuit initiated by Elizabeth Tilton's husband. In the end, Henry was vindicated, although in all likelihood he had had some kind of intimate relationship with Elizabeth.

While weathering the strain of this scandal, Stowe experienced another great personal blow. Her son Fred, still in constant pain from his war injury, was unable to stop drinking. Feeling he was dishonoring his family, he boarded a ship bound for San Francisco and simply disappeared. Stowe never learned what happened to her troubled son.

SPEAKING TO HER READERS

In the spring of 1872, Stowe finally received some good news. The American Literary Bureau of Boston wanted to hire her to do a series of readings from her books in locations throughout New England. In the past, Stowe, as a woman, had not been allowed to speak to large groups. But recently, the women's rights movement had changed the rules of conduct for public

In her lifetime, Stowe influenced people from all walks of life, from government officials to nobility to the oppressed. She was honored not only as a best-selling author but also as a great humanitarian. In her final years, ill health kept her confined to her home in Hartford, Connecticut. There, Stowe welcomed a steady stream of visitors, including family, friends, and literary admirers.

female figures such as Stowe. She was delighted to take on the speaking tour. It would not only earn her a fair amount of money in speaker fees, but would also be an excellent way of promoting her books. Perhaps even more gratifying, it would place her alongside popular male speakers such as writer and philosopher Ralph Waldo Emerson and poet Oliver Wendell Holmes.

With all her expenses paid, Stowe found she loved traveling from engagement to engagement. In a letter home, she wrote, "The fatigue of excitement & all lessens as I get accustomed to it & the fatigue of railroad travel seems to do me good I never sleep better than after a long days ride." The next year she agreed to another lecture tour, this time through the American Midwest. At each stop, old friends and neighbors from her Cincinnati days came out to greet her.

Her audiences were equally excited to see the famous author. A reviewer for the *Pittsburgh Gazette* wrote that her performance "could hardly be called a reading. It was recitative and she seldom glanced at the book. Her voice betrayed the veritable Yankee twang. . . . Her voice is low, just tinged in the slightest with huskiness, but is quite musical. In manner she was vivacious and gave life to many of the pages, more by suggestive action than by utterances. . . . She seemed perfectly possessed on the stage, and read with easy grace."

THE END OF A LONG LIFE

Stowe considered a tour of Canadian cities, but her writing schedule prevented her from taking it on. In the mid-1870s, she published *Palmetto Leaves*, a collection of essays about Florida, and several volumes of sketches on religious subjects. But more and more, she focused on her family. She supervised a wedding for her daughter Georgiana, who settled in Massachusetts and started a family. After selling Oakholm in 1870, she settled in a smaller home in Hartford, of which Eliza and Hatty managed the upkeep. Stowe's only surviving son, Charley, ended his seafaring and settled in Maine. She was delighted when he decided to return to Hartford with his family. In her later years, she doted on Charley, who like her father, husband, and several of her brothers had become a minister. With a keen interest in her son's career, she sometimes drafted outlines of sermons for him to deliver.

POGANUC PEOPLE

In her final book, *Poganuc People*, Harriet Beecher Stowe looked back to her earliest days. The novel is a loving tribute to her New England childhood. In this excerpt, her heroine, Dolly Cushing—a thinly disguised version of Stowe herself as a girl—copes with a family too busy to give her the attention she craves.

"Our little Dolly was a late autumn chicken, the youngest of ten children, the nursing, rearing and caring for whom had straitened the limited salary of Parson Cushing, of Poganuc Center, and sorely worn on the nerves and strength of the good wife who plied the laboring oar in these performances.

It was Dolly's lot to enter the family at a period when babies were no longer a novelty, when the house was full of the wants and clamors of older children, and the mother at her very wits' end with a confusion of jackets and trousers, soap, candles and groceries, and the endless harassments of making both ends meet which pertain to the lot of a poor country minister's wife. Consequently Dolly was disposed of as she grew up in all those short-hand methods by which children were taught to be the least possible trouble to their elders. She was taught to come when called, and do as she was bid without a question or argument, to be quenched in bed at the earliest possible hour at night,

Stowe spent much of her time visiting with her children and grandchildren. She also invited friends over to readings of new novels. Among her best friends in Hartford was her neighbor, the distinguished humorist and novelist Mark Twain. Even with her social schedule, Stowe was still able to complete one final

and to speak only when spoken to in the presence of her elders. All this was a dismal repression to Dolly, for she was by nature a lively, excitable little thing, bursting with questions that she longed to ask, and with comments and remarks that she burned to make. . . .

Dolly was a robust, healthy little creature, never ailing in any way, and consequently received none of the petting which a more delicate child might have claimed, and the general course of her experience impressed her with the mournful conviction that she was always liable to be in the way—as she commonly was, with her childish curiosity, her burning desire to see and hear and know all that interested the grown people above her. Dolly sometimes felt her littleness and insignificance as quite a burden, and longed to be one of the grown-up people. *They* got civil answers when they asked questions, instead of being told not to talk, and they were not sent to bed the minute it was dark, no matter what pleasant things were going on about them. . . . Being gifted with an active fancy, she sometimes imagined a scene when she should be sick and die, and her father and mother and everybody would cry over her, and there would be a funeral for her as there was for little Julia Cavers, one of her playmates. She could see no drawback to the interest of the scene except that she could not be there to enjoy her own funeral and see how much she was appreciated."

book, *Poganuc People* (1878). An affectionate satire of her child-hood in Litchfield, the book was made up of light sketches based on stories she told to her family. Everyone found them so funny that they convinced her to write them down and publish them.

Calvin's health began to falter, but even into her seven-ties Stowe remained alert enough to still manage her career. She often pushed editors to publish new editions of her older works. She was especially pleased with a new illustrated edi-tion of *Uncle Tom's Cabin* that appeared in 1885. She wrote to a friend, "So pretty a book, at so cheap a price ought to command a sale & from the letters constantly coming to me in every mail I judge the interest in it is unabated."

Her readers were not the only ones who remembered and honored Stowe's literary works. Stowe's peers also celebrated her career during a party hosted by the *Atlantic* on her seventy-first birthday. More than 200 leading lights of the literary world turned out to pay homage to Stowe.

After a series of illnesses, Calvin Stowe died on August 6, 1886. As time passed, Harriet, too, grew frail. Hatty told a friend her mother was so forgetful that her mind was like that of a two- or three-year-old. Yet, in 1893, at a doctor's request, Stowe was able to describe with eloquence the limitations placed upon her by age. She explained without regret that she could no longer read well, although flipping through picture books and listening to music played by friends still gave her great joy. Stowe concluded, "I make no mental effort of any sort my brain is tired out . . . [N]ow I rest me, like a moored boat, rising & falling on the water, with loosened cordage and flapping soil." Finally, two weeks after she turned 85, her mind and body gave out. On July 1, 1896, Harriet Beecher Stowe died peacefully in her bed, surrounded by her half sister Isabella and her children Hatty, Eliza, and Charley.

Stowe's Legacy

At the time of Stowe's death, her books, especially *Uncle Tom's Cabin*, had a sizable, if slowly declining, audience. As late as 1899, *Uncle Tom's Cabin* was still the book most frequently checked out of the New York Public Library. Some literary scholars continued to regard the book as an important American novel. For instance, Barrett Wendell, a professor of English at Harvard University, wrote in his *Literary History of America* (1900) that *Uncle Tom's Cabin* was "a remarkable piece of fiction," whose characters possessed a "pervasive vitality . . . [Y]ou unhesitantly accept them as real."

But more commonly, the literary establishment came to view *Uncle Tom's Cabin* as a significant historical document rather than as a great work of fiction. Some critics showed a remarkable animosity toward Stowe's work, perhaps because they devalued any work that was written by a woman, especially one that attracted a wide, adoring audience. Among literary scholars, a popular book written from a female perspective, almost by definition, had to be bad art. Representative of this idea was Julian Hawthorne, the son of novelist Nathaniel Hawthorne, who viciously attacked *Uncle Tom's Cabin* in his *History of American Literature* (1891): "From the literary point of view, its merit is small, both as to style and characterization. . . . [A] more emotional, impassioned, one-sided book was never written."

CRITICISM FROM THE SOUTH

In the decades following the war, Southerners generally became less critical of *Uncle Tom's Cabin*. But many still complained that the book was inaccurate, although instead of challenging Stowe's representation of the cruelty of slavery, they now focused more on her positive portrayal of African-American characters. No African American, the critics claimed, could be as saintly as Tom or as intelligent as George Harris. These views reflected white Southerners' needs after the war to justify laws that discriminated against ex-slaves on the basis that black people were inherently inferior to white people.

In the early twentieth century, one of Stowe's most vehement critics was Thomas Dixon. A novelist from North Carolina, Dixon began his writing career after attending a dramatic performance of *Uncle Tom's Cabin*. Convinced Stowe had grossly misrepresented the South, he set about righting this supposed wrong by penning a series of astoundingly racist novels, including *The Leopard's Spots* (1902) and *The Clansman* (1905). (*The Clansman* is notorious as the source material of the 1915 film *Birth of a Nation*, which, although recognized as a landmark in film history, has also long been condemned for its racist content.)

In *The Leopard's Spots*, Dixon reworked some of Stowe's characters to present a world in which virtuous whites were under constant siege by vulgar and violent blacks. The novel features Tim Shelby, an ex-slave from *Uncle Tom's Cabin*'s Shelby plantation, who is lynched after trying to kiss a white woman. Dixon's grand villain, like Stowe's, was named Simon Legree. However, in Dixon's reimagining, Legree is not a cruel Yankee plantation owner who beats and ravishes his slaves, but instead is an evil Northerner intent on trying to place African Americans in positions of political power in the South.

TOM SHOWS

Early twentieth-century African-American leaders frequently praised *Uncle Tom's Cabin*. W.E.B. DuBois, Booker T. Washington, and Charles Chestnutt all referred to the novel with affection and respect. But they emphasized its role in drawing support for abolition, ignoring disturbing elements of Stowe's portrayals of African Americans. Many African Americans objected to Stowe's black characters, particularly Uncle Tom, who in his passive piety refuses to resist his master, even as he is being beaten to death. Even more blacks, however, were offended by the characters as they were interpreted in performances of the novel.

Soon after the publication of *Uncle Tom's Cabin*, "Tom Shows" were performed throughout the North. Stowe had nothing to do with these productions. She was somewhat uneasy about the theater in general, because in her religious upbringing, theatrical productions were looked upon as dangerously frivolous entertainments. Stowe also did not profit from the proliferation of Tom Shows. At the time, U.S. laws did not provide a book's copyright holder with creative control over or a financial stake in dramatic interpretations of the work. A theater company could legally adapt any book however it saw fit, without offering the original author a cent of compensation.

After the Civil War, Tom Shows only grew in popularity. They were often marketed as family entertainment. One

Tom Shows, which were stage plays and musicals based on *Uncle Tom's Cabin*, were popular with American audiences from the 1850s to the early 1900s. Although the book was a best seller, far more people saw these stage plays than read the book. While some shows faithfully reflected Stowe's antislavery politics, others were little more than minstrel shows (shows that stereotyped and lampooned blacks).

advertisement for an 1866 show touted its educational aspects: "Take the children and give them an ideal and lasting lesson in American history. It is delightful, wonderful, instructive and moral."

Many shows were amateur affairs, staged by poor actors who walked on foot from town to town. They might put on their play in a tent or a barn with props rented from locals. But especially in the late nineteenth and early twentieth century, some Tom Shows were elaborate stage productions. Usually performed only in large cities, these shows competed with one another to stand out, offering more and more thrilling stage effects to bring in an audience. One featured live alligators snapping at Eliza's heels during her dramatic escape. Another strapped invisible wires to the actress playing Eva so that at the end of her deathbed scene she could appear to ascend to heaven. According to Thomas F. Gossett's book *Uncle Tom's Cabin and American Culture* (1985), one company sold its 1902 season by boasting about the astounding number of people and creatures the audience would see on stage: "eighty people, thirty ponies, horses, donkeys, mules and oxen, fifteen ferocious man-eating bloodhounds, and three musical groups—a twenty-piece silver cornet band and orchestra, a fourteen-man genuine African male drum and fife corps, and a twelve-girl creole drum and bugle corps."

PERFORMING STEREOTYPES

Tom Shows were a phenomenon unlike anything seen before or since in American popular culture. In 1902 alone, about 1.5 million Americans saw a Tom Show. Ten years later, Charles Stowe estimated that there had been at least 250,000 productions of *Uncle Tom's Cabin* staged in the United States. Given the number of Tom Shows performed, over time most Americans did not learn about Uncle Tom, Little Eva, or the Harris family by reading Stowe's novel; they learned the story of *Uncle Tom's Cabin* from what they saw on stage.

What they saw on stage was often very different from what Stowe had put on the page. The Tom Shows produced soon after her book's publication usually made some attempt to remain faithful to Stowe's book. But as time passed, the productions increasingly ignored the author's antislavery theme. The dignity and nobility she imbued in her African-American characters were lost. Instead, they were played to elicit cheap laughs or meaningless tears from the audience. Usually the parts of African Americans were played by whites in blackface—a style of theatrical makeup in which the skin is darkened with burnt cork or shoe polish. Most Tom Shows essentially became minstrel shows, entertainments featuring skits, music, and dancing that ridiculed African Americans and their culture.

UNCLE TOM IN ADVERTISING

In the early twentieth century, Tom Shows were a very familiar part of American culture. It is hardly surprising that advertisers took advantage of their popularity and used the shows' characters to try to sell their products. (A gallery of *Uncle Tom*-themed advertisements is featured on the online exhibit "*Uncle Tom's Cabin* & American Culture" at http://www.iath.virginia.edu/utc/tomituds/toadsf.html.)

Topsy, Stowe's mischievous slave girl, was often seen in advertisements for guilty pleasures, probably because in the Tom Shows she was played as a comic figure. For instance, in 1900, Wellmann & Dwire Tobacco advertised "Topsy Tobacco," with an image of Topsy smoking a pipe captioned with "I is so Wicked!" Thirty years later, she was used to sell Topsy Honey Dairy Drink, a chocolate beverage flavored with honey. Some advertisements featured both naughty Topsy and angelic Eva, most likely due to the popularity of a musical titled "Topsy and Eva" during the 1920s and 1930s. Representative of these ads was one from 1940, which trumped six new desserts—three "brunette" ones (presumably chocolate flavored) called Topsies and three "blonde" ones (presumably vanilla flavored) called Evas.

When Uncle Tom appeared in advertisements, he was usually shown as an elderly man, as he generally was in the Tom Shows. His image was used to hock practical foods such as Cream of Wheat and Uncle Tom Health Food, a cereal laxative

FILMING *UNCLE TOM*

The popularity of Tom Shows declined after 1910, although a few were staged as late as the 1950s. The decline did not occur not because Americans had taken a sudden dislike toward Tom

that a 1915 advertisement described as "rich in protein, fat, nitrogen, free extract, and other parts essential in life."

In the 1930s, the Post Cereal Company licensed Walt Disney's Mickey and Minnie Mouse to sell its "Post Toasties." The promotion encouraged children to collect paper images of the cartoon mice depicting Stowe's characters, which they could use to put on their own Tom Shows. Mickey appeared as both Uncle Tom and Topsy, while Minnie took on the role of Eva.

Perhaps the oddest advertisement drawing from *Uncle Tom's Cabin* was one that promoted the very idea of advertisement itself. In 1934, the advertisement agency J. Walter Thompson Company placed a full-page ad in *Fortune* magazine to tout its services. Next to an image of Tom and Eva, the copy read, "If *Uncle Tom's Cabin* is not a great literary work, at least it is the shrewdest piece of selling ever written." The ad went on to explain that by appealing to the emotions of its readers, the novel "made . . . the end of slavery, inevitable." The agency promised its clients the same type of emotional sales pitch, ensuring their success in the marketplace. As crude as most *Uncle Tom's Cabin*-themed advertisements were, the Thompson Company represented something of a low point. Without shame, it equated persuading Americans to reject slavery as a grave moral wrong with convincing consumers to try out a tastier toothpaste or a smoother cigarette.

Shows (although the format was starting to feel dated). Instead, the market for traveling shows decreased in the wake of a new type of entertainment—movies. For a time, however, the movies did keep Tom Shows alive by filming versions of *Uncle Tom's Cabin* based on them. Between 1903 and 1927, nine movies were made of *Uncle Tom's Cabin*, making it the most filmed book in all of the twentieth century.

The 1927 version was particularly notable. It was the third-most expensive silent movie ever made in America. To protect this vast investment, the movie company held special advance screenings in the South to make sure the movie would be acceptable to a Southern audience. Based on the feedback, the studio cut everything that Southern viewers found objectionable. What was left would have stunned Stowe: This *Uncle Tom's Cabin* was a lavish celebration of antebellum Southern culture, rather than the savage critique of it that she had created.

In the film, Uncle Tom was played not by a white man in blackface, but by an African-American actor named James B. Lowe. Lowe was the film studio's second choice. The first actor cast in the part was Charles Gilpin, who had just played the lead in the classic Eugene O'Neill stage drama *The Emperor Jones* (1920). Gilpin was offered $1,000 a week to play Uncle Tom, but even that exorbitant sum was not enough for him in the end. When the director insisted he play the Uncle Tom as completely submissive to whites, Gilpin walked off the set in disgust.

"UNCLE TOM" BECOMES AN INSULT

Gilpin's distaste with the popular portrayals of Uncle Tom was not uncommon among African Americans of the 1920s. Largely because of the Tom Shows, "Uncle Tom" had become a term for any black who debased himself and sold out other blacks in order to curry favor with whites. The "Uncle Tom" stereotype was quite different from Stowe's character. Her Tom was strong and noble, a man of enormous faith and courage. While he came to the aid of whites (often merely by the example of his powerful Christian piety), he also protected his fellow slaves. In fact, his master beat him to death because he refused to give up the hiding place of two slaves who were plotting to escape.

Even so, being called an Uncle Tom eventually became a badge of shame. For instance, as noted by Gossett, African-American leader Marcus Garvey in 1920 declared that "Uncle Tom . . . has got to go and his place must be taken by the new leader of the Negro race." Similarly, in the 1920s, when the African-American train porters working for Pullman company tried to organize a union, they called any porter too timid to join the cause an "Uncle Tom."

The term was so powerful as an insult that it tainted Stowe's novel. Fewer and fewer people read or talked about her classic. In 1944, when a movie studio announced plans to film a new version of *Uncle Tom's Cabin* as a vehicle for actress Lena Horne, the very idea created a firestorm of criticism. Faced by a protest by the National Association for the Advancement of Colored People, the studio immediately abandoned the film project.

ELLISON, WRIGHT, AND BALDWIN ON STOWE

In the mid-twentieth century, a hatred of *Uncle Tom's Cabin* helped fuel the work of some of the greatest African-American writers. Ralph Ellison traced the origin of his novel *The Invisible Man* (1952) to a poster he saw advertising a Tom Show in a small Vermont town in 1945. "I had thought such entertainment a thing of the past," Ellison explained in the introduction to a 1990 edition of his novel, "but there in a quiet northern village it was alive and kicking, with Eliza frantically slipping and sliding on the ice, still trying—and that during World War II!—to escape the slavering hounds." His revulsion helped inspire his groundbreaking novel, which offers a surrealistic examination of the African-American experience in the first half of the twentieth century.

In the twentieth century, novels began to confront prejudices, stereotypes, and racial mythologies and were used to counter previous romanticized notions of plantation life. Richard Wright's *Uncle Tom's Children*, a collection of short stories largely based on Wright's own life, focused on racial oppression from the black person's point of view and helped to redefine the black experience.

Author Richard Wright was even more explicit about Stowe's impact on his work. He titled his first collection of stories *Uncle Tom's Children* (1938). In its epigraph, he wrote,

"The post Civil War household word among Negroes—'He's an Uncle Tom!' . . . has been supplanted by a new word from another generation which says 'Uncle Tom is dead!'"

Wright later regretted that, in setting out to distance himself from Stowe and her novel, he had inadvertently written stories that, like her great work, were designed to make the reader cry. In his 1940 essay "How Bigger Was Born," he bemoaned that he had "written a book which even bankers' daughters could read and weep over and feel good about." In his first novel, he set out to create a vision of the struggles of African-American men "so hard and deep that [readers] would have to face it without the consolation of tears." The result was the classic *Native Son* (1940), whose rapist-murderer protagonist, Bigger Thomas, is consciously crafted as an anti-Uncle Tom. Wright even replicates the Little Eva deathbed scene, but in his version, Bigger Thomas murders Wright's anti-Eva character, a drunken rich woman named Mary Dalton.

Wright's take on Stowe inspired still another great African-American writer, James Baldwin. In his famous 1949 essay, "Everybody's Protest Novel," Baldwin wrote, "Below the surface of [*Native Son*] there lies, as it seems to me, a continuation, a complement of that monstrous legend it was written to destroy. Bigger is Uncle Tom's descendant, flesh of his flesh, so exactly opposite a portrait that, when the books are placed together, it seems that the contemporary Negro novelist and the dead New England woman are locked together in a deadly, timeless battle; the one uttering merciless exhortations, the other shouting curses."

DISMISSING STOWE'S WORK

White critics of the era also attacked Stowe's "monstrous legend," none did so with as much passion as novelist J.C. Furnas. He devoted an entire book, *Goodbye to Uncle Tom* (1956), to blaming Stowe for the long, bitter history of American racism since the Civil War: "As her work soaked into the common mind, fostering cheap sagacity about alleged racial traits down to our own day and affecting millions who have never read Uncle Tom or seen a Tom-show, it has sadly clogged the efforts of modern good will, acting on sounder information, to persuade people that this kind of racist idea does not hold water."

For the most part, however, the arbiters of American literary taste in the mid-twentieth century did not deride Stowe so much as pretend that she did not exist. Her literary reputation (or lack of one) was largely set in motion by F. O. Matthiessen's *American Renaissance* (1941), a hugely influential literary study. It argued that the years between 1850 and 1855 saw the

HUCK FINN AND UNCLE TOM

By the 1990s, many scholars had reexamined *Uncle Tom's Cabin*, recognizing for the first time in many decades that the novel was important not just for its role in U.S. history, but also for its place in American literature. Novelist Jane Smiley further popularized this view in her essay "Say It Ain't So, Huck," which appeared in the January 1996 issue of *Harper's Magazine*. In her essay, Smiley described her experience rereading Mark Twain's *The Adventures of Huckleberry Finn* (1884) for the first time since junior high school. She was stunned by her reaction to this unquestioned classic. Rather than seeing it as the great American novel about race, she was disturbed by the book's treatment of its primary African-American character—Jim, a slave who is trying to escape to freedom. She faults both Huckleberry Finn and his creator for not caring enough about Jim and his fate: "[N]either Huck not Twain takes Jim's desire for freedom at production of many of the greatest masterworks of American literature, including novels by Herman Melville and Nathaniel Hawthorne. The book, however, did not discuss *Uncle Tom's Cabin*, the most popular and influential American novel published during those years. In the mid-twentieth century, if literary scholars mentioned Stowe's novel at all, it was usually to mock it as the epitome of soppy sentimentalism.

REEVALUATING *UNCLE TOM'S CABIN*

Here and there, a few important scholars, notably Edmund Wilson and Leslie Fiedler, came to Stowe's defense. But it was not

all seriously; that is, they do not accord it the respect that a man's passion deserves." Smiley concludes her essay by arguing that Harriet Beecher Stowe's masterpiece is at least, if not more, worthy of a place in the American literary canon:

> "I would rather my children read *Uncle Tom's Cabin*, even though it is far more vivid in its depiction of cruelty than *Huck Finn*, and this is because Stowe's novel is clearly and unmistakably a tragedy. No whitewash, no secrets, but evil, suffering, imagination, endurance, and redemption—just like life. Like little Eva, who eagerly but fearfully listens to the stories of the slaves that her family tries to keep from her, our children want to know what is going on, what has gone on, and what we intend to do about it. If 'great' literature has any purpose, it is to help us face up to our responsibilities instead of enabling us to avoid them once again by lighting out for the territory."

until the late 1970s and 1980s that she and her works were fully reexamined. Scholars schooled in feminist and African-American studies led this reassessment, once again seeing the power in *Uncle Tom's Cabin* that had had such a profound impact on its original readers. Particularly notable was the essay "Sentimental Power: *Uncle Tom's Cabin* and the Politics of Literary History" by Jane P. Tompkins. Tompkins argued that *Uncle Tom's Cabin*'s appeal to the emotions—its much maligned sentimentality— was a strength, not a weakness, of the book. Tompkins claimed this feature allowed the novel to offer a "critique of American society far more devastating than any delivered by better-known critics such as Hawthorne and Melville."

In recent years, the literary study of Stowe's works has exploded. Most of it has concentrated on *Uncle Tom's Cabin*, but some scholars have also started examining her other works, particularly noting her contributions to such genres as social satire and travel writing. For a time in the mid-twentieth century, *Uncle Tom's Cabin* was out of print. It is now available in dozens of editions and has become a staple of the curriculum in both high schools and universities across the United States.

Even with its newfound popularity, *Uncle Tom's Cabin* remains a difficult book for many to embrace. Its sentimental style is off-putting to some contemporary readers. Its view of relations between whites and blacks, so progressive in its day, strikes a modern audience as naïve at best and racist at worst. Its shameless history on the stage has left such a cultural residue on the words "Uncle Tom" alone that it remains a struggle to read Stowe's story with a clear, unbiased eye. Yet, Stowe's work has left an indelible mark on American history and culture, an influence extending over more than a century and a half, since its first publication so inflamed the hearts and minds of a nation. As African-American novelist and scholar Charles Johnson explained in his introduction of a 2002 edition of *Uncle Tom's Cabin,* "we may love or hate [it], admire or despise [it], defend or reject [it], in whole or in part. It is nonetheless a story that so permeates white popular and literary culture, and sits so high astride nineteenth-century American fiction, that it simply can never be ignored."

1811 Harriet Elizabeth Beecher is born in Litchfield, Connecticut.

1824 Beecher begins attending the Hartford Female Seminary founded by her sister Catharine.

1832 Beecher moves to Cincinnati, Ohio, after her father Lyman is named president of the Lane Theological Seminary.

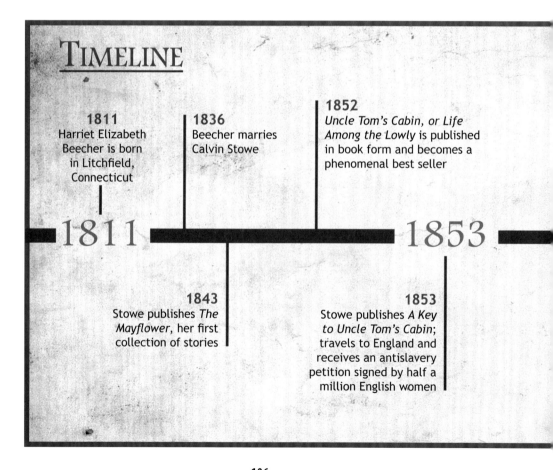

TIMELINE

1811
Harriet Elizabeth Beecher is born in Litchfield, Connecticut

1836
Beecher marries Calvin Stowe

1852
Uncle Tom's Cabin, or Life Among the Lowly is published in book form and becomes a phenomenal best seller

1811 — **1853**

1843
Stowe publishes *The Mayflower*, her first collection of stories

1853
Stowe publishes *A Key to Uncle Tom's Cabin*; travels to England and receives an antislavery petition signed by half a million English women

1833 Beecher publishes the successful textbook *Primary Geography for Children*.

1836 Beecher marries Calvin Stowe, a professor at the Lane Theological Seminary.

1839 Harriet Beecher Stowe begins publishing stories in national magazines, such as *Godey's Lady's Book*.

1843 Stowe publishes *The Mayflower*, her first collection of stories.

1849 Stowe mourns the death of her sixth child, Samuel Charles, during a cholera epidemic.

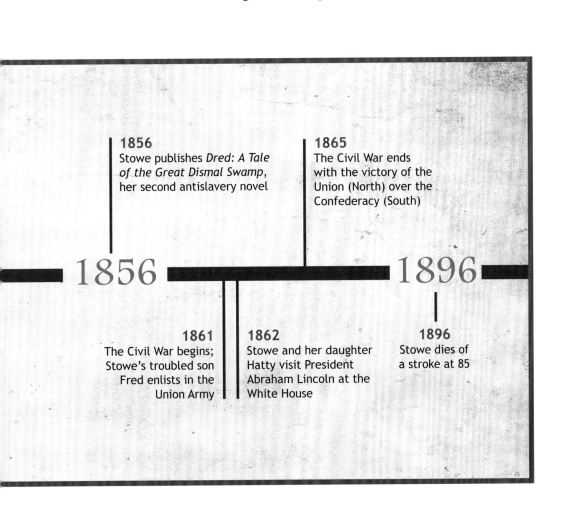

1856
Stowe publishes *Dred: A Tale of the Great Dismal Swamp*, her second antislavery novel

1865
The Civil War ends with the victory of the Union (North) over the Confederacy (South)

1856

1896

1861
The Civil War begins; Stowe's troubled son Fred enlists in the Union Army

1862
Stowe and her daughter Hatty visit President Abraham Lincoln at the White House

1896
Stowe dies of a stroke at 85

1850   Stowe moves to Brunswick, Maine, after her husband takes a job at Bowdoin College.

1851   The *National Era* begins serializing Stowe's *Uncle Tom's Cabin, or Life Among the Lowly.*

1852   *Uncle Tom's Cabin* is published in book form and becomes a phenomenal best seller.

1853   Stowe publishes *A Key to Uncle Tom's Cabin* as a defense to criticism of her book; Stowe travels to England and receives an antislavery petition signed by half a million English women.

1856   Stowe publishes *Dred: A Tale of the Great Dismal Swamp*, her second antislavery novel.

1857   Stowe's son Henry dies in a drowning accident.

1861   The Civil War begins; Stowe's troubled son Fred enlists in the Union Army.

1862   Stowe publishes *The Pearl of Orr's Island* and *Agnes of Sorrento*; Stowe and her daughter Hatty visit President Abraham Lincoln at the White House.

1864   The Stowes move to Oakholm, a mansion in Hartford, Connecticut.

1865   The Civil War ends with the victory of the Union (North) over the Confederacy (South).

1867   Stowe purchases a winter home in Mandarin, Florida.

1870   Stowe publishes *Lady Byron Vindicated*, which critics brand as vulgar.

1878   Stowe's final novel, *Poganuc People*, based on her childhood in New England, is published.

1896   Stowe, after years of ill health, dies of a stroke at 85.

GLOSSARY

abolitionism   Nineteenth-century movement to end slavery in the United States

antebellum   Occurring prior to the Civil War

anti-Tom novels   Novels written largely by Southerners intended to challenge the view of slavery presented in *Uncle Tom's Cabin*

colonization   Early nineteenth-century policy that advocated sending freed African-American slaves to live in the African country of Liberia

Confederacy   Southern states that seceded from and fought against the Union during the Civil War

Confederate States of America   Government formed by the Southern states that seceded from the United States between 1861 and 1865

Emancipation Proclamation   Executive order, issued by President Abraham Lincoln on January 1, 1863, that freed all slaves in the Confederate States of America

free states   U.S. states in which slavery was illegal prior to the Civil War

Fugitive Slave Law   1850 federal law that prohibited all Americans from aiding fugitive slaves

secede   To withdraw from a political state or organization

serial   Literary work, especially a novel, published in installments in a newspaper or magazine

slave states   U.S. states in which slavery was legal prior to the Civil War

Tom Shows   Stage productions of *Uncle Tom's Cabin*, popular in the late nineteenth century and early twentieth century, that often presented stereotyped African-American characters

Uncle Tom   Title character of *Uncle Tom's Cabin*, more recently used as an insulting term for an African American who degrades himself or other African Americans in order to win the favor of whites

Underground Railroad   Network of safe houses established to help fugitive slaves escape to freedom in free states or in Canada

Union   Northern states that remained loyal to the United States and fought against the Confederacy during the Civil War

BIBLIOGRAPHY

Ammons, Elizabeth. *Harriet Beecher Stowe's Uncle Tom's Cabin: A Casebook*. New York: Oxford University Press, 2007.

Hedrick, Joan D. *Harriet Beecher Stowe: A Life*. New York: Oxford University Press, 1994.

McFarland, Philip. *Loves of Harriet Beecher Stowe*. New York: Grove Press, 2007.

Robbins, Sarah. *The Cambridge Introduction to Harriet Beecher Stowe*. New York: Cambridge University Press, 2007.

Rugoff, Milton. *The Beechers: An American Family in the Nineteenth Century*. New York: Harper & Row, 1981.

Stowe, Charles Edward. *Life of Harriet Beecher Stowe, Compiled from Her Letters and Journals*. Boston, Mass.: Houghton, Mifflin and Co., 1889.

Stowe, Harriet Beecher. *The Annotated Uncle Tom's Cabin*. Edited with an introduction and notes by Henry Louis Gates, Jr., and Hollis Robbins. New York: W.W. Norton, 2007.

Sundquist, Eric J. *New Essays on Uncle Tom's Cabin*. New York: Cambridge University Press, 1986.

Weinstein, Cindy. *The Cambridge Companion to Harriet Beecher Stowe*. New York: Cambridge University Press, 2004.

FURTHER RESOURCES

BOOKS

Altman, Linda Jacobs. *Slavery and Abolition in American History*. Berkeley Heights, NJ: Enslow Publishers, 1999.

Clinton, Catherine. *The Civil War: An Illustrated History*. New York: Scholastic, 2004.

Haugen, Brenda. *Harriet Beecher Stowe: Author and Advocate*. Minneapolis, Minn.: Compass Point Books, 2005.

Robbins, Sarah. *The Cambridge Introduction to Harriet Beecher Stowe*. New York: Cambridge University Press, 2007.

Sigerman, Harriet. *Laborers for Liberty: American Women 1865–1890*. New York: Oxford University Press, 1998.

———. *An Unfinished Battle: American Women 1848–1865*. New York: Oxford University Press, 1998.

Stowe, Harriet Beecher. *The Annotated Uncle Tom's Cabin*. Edited with an introduction and notes by Henry Louis Gates, Jr., and Hollis Robbins. New York: W.W. Norton, 2006.

Tackach, James. *Uncle Tom's Cabin: Indictment of Slavery*. San Diego: Lucent Books, 2000.

WEB SITES

The African-American Mosaic: Abolition
http://www.loc.gov/exhibits/african/afam005.html
This Library of Congress Resource Guide offers information about the origins and significance of the American abolition movement.

African-American Odyssey: Abolition, Antislavery Movements, and the Rise of the Sectional Controversy
http://lcweb2.loc.gov/ammem/aaohtml/exhibit/aopart3.html

This site discusses the American abolition and antislavery movements of the nineteenth century through period documents preserved by the Library of Congress.

The Classic Text: Harriet Beecher Stowe
http://www.uwm.edu/Library/special/exhibits/clastext/ clspg149.htm

This site, sponsored by the University of Wisconsin–Milwaukee, explores the publication history and social and cultural impact of *Uncle Tom's Cabin* and other works by Stowe.

Harriet Beecher Stowe Center
http://www.harrietbeecherstowecenter.org

Located in Stowe's house in Hartford, Connecticut, the Harriet Beecher Stowe Center offers on its Web site a selection of brief essays about Stowe's life and times.

"I Will Be Heard!": Abolitionism in America
http://rmc.library.cornell.edu/abolitionism

This online exhibit, created by the Cornell University Library, provides a comprehensive introduction to abolitionism and contains a section devoted to *Uncle Tom's Cabin.*

A Novel Idea: *Uncle Tom's Cabin*
http://www.lib.virginia.edu/small/exhibits/theatre/idea_ cabin.html

Operated by the University of Virginia Library, this site devoted to the American theater uses posters and playbills to illustrate the history of stage plays based on *Uncle Tom's Cabin.*

Uncle Tom's Cabin & American Culture
http://www.iath.virginia.edu/utc

This valuable online exhibit, curated by Professor Stephen Railton of the University of Virginia, features essays and illustrations that explore the influence of *Uncle Tom's Cabin* on American history and culture.

PICTURE CREDITS

❧ INDEX ❧

ABOUT THE AUTHOR

LIZ SONNEBORN is a writer living in Brooklyn, New York. A graduate of Swarthmore College, she has written more than 70 books for children and adults, including *The American West*, *The Gold Rush*, *A to Z of American Indian Women*, *The Mexican-American War*, *Benedict Arnold*, and *Chronology of American Indian History*.